D0908361

Lafcadio Hearn and the Vision of Japan

Parallax Re-visions of Culture and Society

Stephen G. Nichols, Gerald Prince, and Wendy Steiner,
Series Editors

Lafcadio Hearn, age thirty-nine, shortly before his departure for Japan. Photograph by Frederick Gutekunst, 1889. *Courtesy of the Lafcadio Hearn Collection, Rare Books Section, Howard-Tilton Memorial Library, Tulane University.*

CARL DAWSON

Lafcadio Hearn and the Vision of Japan

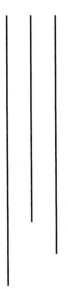

The Johns Hopkins University Press
Baltimore and London

© 1992 The Johns Hopkins University Press
All rights reserved
Printed in the United States of America

The Johns Hopkins University Press
701 West 40th Street
Baltimore, Maryland 21211-2190
The Johns Hopkins Press Ltd., London

The paper used in this book meets the minimum requirements of the
American National Standard for Information Sciences—Permanence of
Paper for Printed Library Materials, ANSI Z39.48-1984.

Library of Congress Cataloging-in-Publication Data

Dawson, Carl.
  Lafcadio Hearn and the vision of Japan / Carl Dawson.
    p.   cm. — (Parallax : re-visions of culture and society)
  Includes bibliographical references and index.
  ISBN 0-8018-4372-3 (alk. paper)
  1. Hearn, Lafcadio, 1850–1904—Homes and haunts—Japan.
2. Hearn, Lafcadio, 1850–1904—Knowledge—Japan.   3. Authors,
American—19th century—Biography.   4. Americans—Japan—
History—19th century.   5. Japan in literature.   6. Japan—
Civilization.   I. Title.   II. Series: Parallax (Baltimore, Md.)
PS1918.D38   1992
813'.4—dc20   91-44785

for Geoffrey and Sarah

Contents

If I want to imagine a fictive nation, I can give it an invented name, treat it declaratively as a novelistic object . . . so as to compromise no real country by my fantasy. . . . I can also—though in no way claiming to represent or to analyze reality itself (these being the major gestures of Western discourse)—isolate somewhere in the world (*faraway*) a certain number of features . . . , and out of these features deliberately form a system. It is this system which I shall call: Japan

—Roland Barthes, *Empire of Signs*

What gives value to travel is fear. It is the fact that, at a certain moment, when we are so far from our own country . . . , we are seized by a vague fear, and an instinctive desire to go back to the protection of old habits. This is the most obvious benefit of travel. At that moment, we are feverish but also porous, so that the slightest touch makes us quiver to the depths of our being. We come across a cascade of light, and there is eternity. . . . If we understand by culture the experience of our most intimate sense—that of eternity—then we travel for culture.

—Albert Camus, *Notebooks, 1935–42*

Preface

I would give anything to be a literary Columbus.
—Lafcadio Hearn

In the spring of 1890, Lafcadio Hearn arrived in Yokohama, Japan. He was thirty-nine years old. His assignment, from *Harper's Magazine*, called for a series of articles about Japanese life and customs. Within a few weeks Hearn had severed relations with his editor, quarreled with his photographer, and found himself without friends or money in an alien land. Sudden and apparently overwhelming crises were for Lafcadio Hearn signs of a recurrent pattern of loss and abandonment, as predictable as they were self-made. He had been destitute before: as a boy in London, as a teenager in New York and Cincinnati, and as a man in New Orleans and Martinique. Hearn's previous beginnings had all offered a new life, along with escape from unwanted people, lost illusions, or unbearable tedium.

Life in Meiji Japan met two of Hearn's constant needs, for in the last phase of his life until his death in 1904 he found both a home and an audience, loving and hating Japan while establishing himself as its preeminent interpreter for the Western world. In England, America, France, and Germany, readers of Hearn's books and popular articles preferred his accounts to those of an earlier favorite (and a favorite of Hearn himself), Pierre Loti, and to those of scholarly commentators such as Basil Hall Chamberlain.

Other writers might have fuller knowledge or translate better or write more coherent books; no one else gave quite the same assurance of being there. Astounding as it seems, Hearn never really mastered the Japanese language, much as he loved to paint the letters or speak whatever he learned. So it was also not linguistic accuracy that persuaded readers but, rather, Hearn's sympathetic trespass, his authority as a complete witness. Reading Hearn, as the novelist Stefan Zweig suggested, ranked second only to visiting the country.[1]

My own discovery of Hearn came several years ago when planning a trip to Japan. Previously unfamiliar with his Japanese books and their contemporary reputation, I soon recognized that, while Hearn told of a Japan long vanished, he still addressed questions that mattered, still offered uncanny insight into the old-new world he had found.[2] Having said this, I should make my disclaimers. First, I am not a student of Japanese history nor, in any deeply informed way, of its arts and culture. Second, my inability to learn the language has prevented my reading some pertinent studies by Japanese scholars. I can only hope that areas of strength may offset areas of weakness. In any case, it will be clear that I am writing at most indirectly about late nineteenth-century Japan and that my concerns are with the Japan Hearn imagined for his readers, the qualities of his exiled life, and the struggle he articulated (and embodied) in coming to terms with a foreign culture.

Hearn's journey to Japan, almost a century before my own, spoke with an urgency I could not resist. This was not simply because he served to guide my own encounters or because I, too, would be teaching Japanese undergraduates, in part about Hearn himself. I read this man's books with a sense of déjà vu, with the growing recognition that his depiction of Japan, idiosyncratic as it was, drew on the assumptions of his Western contemporaries and paralleled the self-histories I had written about in *Prophets of Past Time*, a study of turn-of-the-century autobiographers.[3] Hearn's commitment to ideas of collective and racial

memories, his linking of memory with evolutionary principles, and his fascination with divided personalities recalled George Moore and Samuel Butler, Edmund Gosse
and William Butler Yeats, writers as different from one
another as they were from Hearn but who shared a profound interest in the ways we remember.

Hearn reflected his generation, the fin-de-siècle generation, from which—physically and temperamentally—he
also stood apart. His adult years had been spent mainly in
the United States, and not even there had he lived near the
center of literary activities. Like a case history out of Max
Nordau's contemporary diatribe against "degeneration,"
the decadence of the fin de siècle, he had the physical lia-
bilities and mental or emotional excesses that Nordau
considered emblematic of a troubled civilization.[4] Hearn
prided himself on his kinship with "decadent" and "sen-
sualist" writers, especially the French, but, as his homage
to duty, fidelity, and honor suggest, he would have disappointed a determined aesthete.

Hearn's reading interests make clear how far his values
(or opinions) went beyond the predictable. He brought to
Japan a passion for reading, most of it random and unconnected to any of the inadequate schooling he had endured
as a boy. He knew psychologists such as James Sully, scientific spokesmen such as Thomas Henry Huxley, and contemporary novelists such as Rudyard Kipling and Henry
James. The classics engrossed him, as did folklore, ghost
stories, and modern poetry. He translated French writers
from Théophile Gautier to Guy de Maupassant, wrote articles about recent scientific and technological advances,
and engaged himself with everything from public hangings
to the economics of sweatshops. However much his reporting demanded of him, he always devoted his free time to
books, sharing enthusiasms with friends and with the face-
less readers of his newspaper and magazine articles.

Hearn's main reading passion competed even more with
late-century aesthetic and decadent assumptions. Since
the 1880s he had become a strong advocate of Herbert

Spencer, "the wisest man in the world,"[5] whose faults he scarcely recognized and whose virtues he espoused in almost any forum available to him. Spencer enjoyed great vogue in late nineteenth-century America, seeming to the newly rich entrepreneurs a spokesman for unbridled economic liberties and for endless "progress." As a follower of Lamarck rather than Darwin, Spencer insisted on "inherited characteristics," learned qualities that could be passed on from generation to generation and that allowed superior men and women to exploit their natural strengths. In spite of his own physical weakness, not to mention several fortuitous inheritances, Spencer believed that individuals should be strong enough to fend for themselves; it was he who coined the phrase "survival of the fittest." Hearn, who struggled throughout most of his life, candidly admitted that he was "not among the 'fittest.'"[6]

Vacillating on questions of progress and social advancement, Hearn apparently did subscribe to Spencer's theories of "force," which he saw, in combination with Schopenhauer's "will," not only as an explanation of geological and biological change but also as a key to understanding the development of races and civilizations. With no sense of contradictory purposes, Hearn quotes Spencer's arrogant, albeit solicited, advice to Japanese officials about goals for their country—even though Spencer spoke categorically against some of Hearn's deepest convictions, among them the desirability of intermarriage between races. Like their American counterparts, Japanese business and political leaders appreciated Spencer, no doubt because he promised a great future for the physically and intellectually strong. Ironically, in the last decades of the century intellectuals in both England and America (William James prominent among them) found Spencer's science wanting, his intellectual schemes simplistic.

Hearn admired Spencer for several reasons. Above all, he preferred evolutionary principles that implied purpose or direction, that seemed more humanistic than those of Darwin. Then, too, he stood in awe of an encyclopedic and synthetic thinker, of someone who pioneered in several fields (notably sociology and psychology) and wrote aggressively about many others. In his "synthetic philosophy," Spencer offered a unifying theory of knowledge,[7] or at the least a framework for Hearn's self-education, and Hearn could take pleasure in the fact that Spencer himself was largely self-educated. He read Spencer's books in an obviously personal way. Spencer's notions about "organic memory," for example, provided Hearn with a way of understanding both history and literature, in which collective memories constantly inform present thinking. At first convinced that Spencer had pushed "Orientalism" out of his mind, he later equated Spencer's theories of "remembering" with Buddhist philosophy, which had long intrigued him and became an obsession during his years in Japan.

Hearn's education reflected the piecemeal quality of the life he lived. Some of his readers have damned him for the errors of his life; some have found its exotic nature essential to his writing. George Gould, a Philadelphia doctor and a onetime friend, published a slashing book in which the puny and demonic Hearn exemplifies all the sins of decadence cataloged by Max Nordau:

He has been spoken of as a "great man," which of course he was not. . . . Deprived by nature, by the necessities of his life, or by conscious intention, of religion, morality, scholarship, magnanimity, loyalty, character, benevolence, and other constituents of personal greatness, it is more than folly to place him thus before the world.[8]

Sadly, Hearn himself shared Gould's assessment. Perhaps in innocence, perhaps self-protectively, he often listed his faults to friends before accusing them of attacking him. When denied the stimulus of hatred, which he at once dreaded and invited, he admitted to feeling inert or uncreative: "Unless somebody does or says something horribly mean to me, I can't do certain kinds of work."[9] More often the initiator rather than the victim, Hearn hurt others with abrupt shifts in his affections; he ended friendships as spontaneously as he changed places.

Notwithstanding his mercurial temperament and his readiness to take offense, Hearn kept the allegiance of most rejected friends, who accepted his ambivalences and, unlike George Gould, thought him gentle, compassionate, and brilliant. Friends and strangers alike praised his work, agreeing with Paul Elmer More's early estimate that Hearn's writings present "one of the most extraordinary artistic achievements of modern days."[10]

In the chapters that follow I address the qualities of that achievement, the ways it mattered to Hearn's contemporaries, and the value it may still have for readers interested in the life of the writer himself, in late nineteenth-century travel, or in Western conceptions of Japan. My concern is with Hearn's visions of Japan, which really means the ways that he, as a Westerner of his time, created Japan for audiences in Europe and America.

To enter into Hearn's Japanese books is to appreciate the subtlety of his values as they contrast with unexamined or crassly imperialistic positions of most Western travelers. In this he resembles early modern anthropologists, for example, his contemporary Franz Boas, who delighted in remote cultures. "I am now a true Eskimo," says Boas;[11] Hearn might have said, "I am now a Japanese." Not without misgivings, he actually adopted Japanese citizenship, and, if he never mastered the language, he lived as fully as possible in the ways of native inhabitants.

It may be self-evident that neither Hearn nor Boas truly approximated the people they studied and revered. They came as foreigners, absorbed in the ideas and ideologies of their generation. Only with time and disillusion did Hearn learn to question assumptions about the vast movement of Orientalism,[12] the peculiar complex of politics and racial assumptions that informed, among so many, two of Hearn's favorite authors, Gerard de Nerval on the Middle East and Percival Lowell on China and Japan, and prompted

Hearn's initial love for his adopted and adopting land. During his fourteen years in Japan, Hearn grew progressively skeptical about the country and about his own enthusiasm for it. Still, perhaps no foreigner has ever devoted himself to Japan as he did or so defined himself by its cultural heritage, and certainly none has managed to write powerfully for Western audiences while winning, in later years, generous readers among the Japanese.

Hearn readily admitted his failings as a writer, his sense of responsibilities too large for his powers. Having found little success as a novelist or poet, he had remained a journalist, a translator, an editor, a collector of folklore, and above all a writer of travel impressions. In Japan he applied his skills to a more ambitious type of book, a composite of earlier work with new topics and in a familiar but more elastic form. If not quite autobiography, his books are autobiographical, recounting his observations and self-discovery in pursuit of a seductive and elusive land.

Although Hearn is an unusually distinctive writer, his mannerisms recognizable to anyone who has read his works,[13] he is also, as Gould insisted, something of a chameleon, adjusting to changes of circumstance or discovering new and unpredictable selves in worlds of his own imagining. Without trying to construct a personality for a man who came to insist on the illusion of personality or the impossibility of a discrete self, it should be clear that I think of Hearn as an "author," a person reclaimable over the years and through his texts. At the same time, I share his consciousness of the gulf between the man who writes and the books he produces, and its corollaries: that any attempt at understanding must be provisional and that successful writing, as Bertolt Brecht described it, demands a transition from egocentricity to selflessness.

How Hearn writes is the implicit topic of all my chapters and the central topic of chapters 3 and 4. I turn first to his encounter with Japan, speaking about the emotional and intellectual baggage he brought with him. Then I try to place him in the context of other Westerners—by his time numerous—who sailed from Europe or the west coasts of Canada and the United States to see the Land of the Rising Sun. After discussing Hearn's writings, I consider his role as a mediator between East and West, as a lecturer in Japan on British and American literature. I turn, finally, to his vision of what he called in one essay "the civilization of Japan."

During the writing of this book I have had the support of friends and colleagues at two universities. At the University of New Hampshire, Dean Stuart Palmer and Professor Michael V. DePorte were of great help. To Michael I owe special thanks, not only for his original suggestion that I look at Hearn's writings but also for his generous friendship and interest in my work. At both the University of New Hampshire and the University of Delaware, Chris Fauske has been an astute and helpful reader, sometimes knowing what I wanted to say before I was clear myself. Susan Goodman has read early drafts, and I have borrowed shamelessly from her. Ellen Pifer, Charles Robinson, and Tamara K. Hareven have been supportive colleagues at the University of Delaware. Janet Casey, Christine Volonte, and Meoghan Byrne have been resourceful in providing information and tracking down sources; I thank them for their good humor and patient work.

In Japan professors Yoshio Tsuda, Naoomi Kuratani, Harohide Mori, Yukimasa Hattori, Kenji Zenimoto, and Yoshigoro Shinkai have all been generous with their time, as has Bon Koizumi, great-grandson of Lafcadio Hearn and curator of the Lafcadio Hearn Memorial Museum in Matsue. President Kazuaki Kurozawa, of Shoin Women's University, has been unfailingly supportive; it was with him that I first saw Matsue and the west coast of Japan. Conversations with Francis King, Grant K. Goodman, George E. H. Hughes, Jon C. Hughes, and Louis Allen (at the 1990 Hearn Centennial Festival in Matsue) helped me to come to terms with some of my ideas.

Dean Helen Gouldner of the University of Delaware has made it possible for me to return to Japan and to travel to libraries. Among these, I want particularly to acknowledge the kindness of the staffs at the Huntington Library, the University of New Hampshire Library, the Matsue Municipal Library, the Library of Congress, the Milton S. Eisenhower Library at the Johns Hopkins University, the Shoin Women's University Library, and above all the Morris Library at the University of Delaware and the C. Waller Barrett Collection in the Alderman Library, University of Virginia. Ms. Sylvia Verdun Metzinger, rare books librarian at the Howard-Tilton Memorial Library, Tulane University, has been especially gracious.

My debt to earlier students of Hearn and to writers about Japan should be clear from my notes. P. D. and Ione Perkins's *Lafcadio Hearn: A Bibliography of his Writings*, Beongcheon Yu's fine critical study, *An Ape of Gods: The Art and Thought of Lafcadio Hearn*, various studies (collected in *Discoveries*) by Albert Mordell, biographies by Elizabeth Stevenson and Marcel Robert, and the novelistic biography of Robert A. Rosenstone, *Mirror in the Shrine*, have been especially helpful, as have Yokoyama Toshio's *Japan in the Victorian Mind*, which attends to an earlier era, and Masao Miyoshi's superb *As We Saw Them*, a book focusing on the first Japanese mission to the United States in 1860, which in fact deals with central issues of cultural difference. I have also drawn from Earl R. Miner's unexcelled *The Japanese Tradition in British and American Literature*, Hugh Cortazzi's welcome editions of nineteenth-century writings about Japan, historical studies by Sir G. B. Sansom and Edwin O. Reischauer, literary studies by Donald Keene, cultural studies by Edward Said and Patrick Brantlinger, and anthropological histories by James Clifford and George W. Stocking.[14]

Note on texts: I have used the sixteen-volume set of *The Writings of Lafcadio Hearn* when appropriate, although many of Hearn's writings are only available in separately issued volumes. Except for *Japan: An Attempt at Interpretation*, now out of print, I have cited paperback editions of Hearn's books about Japan, which are more readily accessible than the *Writings*.[15]

Lafcadio Hearn and the Vision of Japan

[1]
The Voyage Out

1   (But where is what I started for so long ago?
    And why is it yet unfound?)
        —Walt Whitman, "Facing West from California"

    His was a world cut off from all standards, except the
    intensity of its own impressions.
        —Ernest Fenollosa on the painter Hokusai

A photograph in the Lafcadio Hearn museum in Matsue, Japan, shows a small man walking away from the camera. His suit is loose and ill fitting, his hat broad brimmed, his arms weighted by a satchel and an old suitcase. With one foot pointing outward and his body slightly bent, the man looks uncertain or off balance as he moves toward the port: Charlie Chaplin as a not quite down-and-out tramp.

Whether or not the photograph offers a historical portrait of the man Lafcadio Hearn, it seems oddly apt. In the first place, it is a photograph of a drawing, a sketch by a man called Weldon, Hearn's traveling companion, rather than a photograph of Hearn himself. Usually avoiding the camera or turning to one side to shield his blind eye, Hearn can be recognized in group photographs as the person looking down or, more characteristically, looking down and away from the intruding lens. Here, with his face turned from the man he resented and would soon ignore entirely, he strides toward the new shore. He had a world to explore and no time for unwanted companions.

The man in the drawing-photograph appears both caricatured and slightly out of focus, a distant reminder from that April morning in 1890 how far away he is—how hard to imagine, let alone to know. Hearn himself, fascinated by the technology of the camera, often described his visual world in terms of drawing and photography, using both as metaphors for personal and ancestral memories. When he thinks of cameras and images developed by the mind, he sees a connection between writing and memory and between memory and human evolution, which links one mind with many, one act of creativity with the development of the species. Through the gathered wisdom of ancestors, who direct our acts of "composition,"[1] we learn emotions such as fear and inherit an awareness of beauty.

Hearn's interest in and experience with cameras (in the French West Indies) may have allowed him, using words of a contemporary reviewer, to photograph "the Japanese soul,"[2] but he became more concerned with intuitive insights than with literal recording. Late in his career he said that "photographs only give us surfaces; and the surfaces of society are constantly changing."[3] An almost compulsive "realist" in his journalism days, he grew at once more particular about his language and more aware of "*an emptiness of language,*" which, as Roland Barthes suggests in his own book about Japan, forces the writer to vacillate in his thinking. Barthes, who equates the process of discovery and writing with satori, the Zen "occurrence," recalls Hearn's struggle to understand himself as he came to terms with the shock of Japan. For Hearn, too, Japan afforded "a situation for writing" that both intensified and made bearable the emptiness of his life.[4]

In Hearn's thinking a personality is always an amalgam, not to say an impossibility, and his own contradictory and elusive qualities exemplified the theory. A New York friend, Ellwood Hendrick, said after his death that "Lafcadio Hearn was a mystery to his friends as he is to us today."[5] The mystery originates, in part, from Hearn's own conviction of a discontinuous self—a self, like the country he came to observe, seen in brief but intense flashes.

I can best approach the mystery by evoking again the

Like his father, Kazuo Koizumi loved to draw. This is an undated crayon portrait of Hearn in his last years. *Courtesy of the Lafcadio Hearn Collection, Rare Books Section, Howard-Tilton Memorial Library, Tulane University.*

drawing of his arrival in Japan. When beginning to write I had remembered a full depiction of the man and his surroundings, with the port of Yokohama behind him, the distant vistas of trees and hills, the "dreamy luminosity over Yokohama bay."[6] None of this occurs in the drawing itself, which offers a sketch of the receding figure with the man's movement suggested by a deft series of lines. I had created in memory what Hearn would describe as the composite visions of other travelers, including those by the intrepid Englishwoman Isabella L. Bird or John La Farge, the American painter; or perhaps I had conjured up the powerful photographs of Felice Beato, who, a generation before Hearn, had studied the traditional ways of the Japanese as Hearn was to do in a different medium.[7] Put another way, I had been involved with the sort of process that preoccupied Hearn, the imagining of physical and historical contexts beyond the suggestion of the eye.

If we accept the small, awkward figure seen by Hearn's traveling companion as Lafcadio Hearn arriving in Yokohama, we can enlarge the portrait. Hearn was once again the solitary, asserting his need to be alone. No self-confident man of business or industry, diplomat or railroad engineer, naval officer or soldier, he was what the photographic image suggests: an almost penniless journalist, unsure about why he was there or what he would do or even, within a matter of weeks, where his next meal would be found. More than Hearn's poverty set him apart. He came to Japan, just as he had earlier gone to Cincinnati and New Orleans, with an open mind as well as empty pockets. He came questioning, without any obvious assumption about his own racial or cultural superiority—perhaps the contrary. Aside from the need to earn a living, he came to learn.

Few people of his generation learned more about Japan, and even fewer were to plunge themselves, as Hearn so wholeheartedly did, into the culture of the land. After a lifetime of wandering and loneliness, Hearn found in Japan a gratifying, if only temporary, sense of belonging. For this reason, he was to see it as it had not been seen, even by astute observers such as Rudyard Kipling or Basil Hall Chamberlain, the English scholar who befriended Hearn and taught him much about Japanese life. Without ever coming close to Chamberlain's knowledge of Japanese, he learned to live in Japan with an informed intuition of its ways, its people, and its arts.

But what was the story behind the improvident-looking figure disembarking in Yokohama a hundred years ago? The subject of several biographies and at least two biographical novels, Hearn's life lends itself to exaggeration and parody.[8] This is how a Ripley's "Believe It or Not" newspaper column summed it up in 1933:

Lafcadio Hearn, distinguished author, was born in the Ionian Islands of a Greek mother and Irish father. He was raised in Wales, worked in the United States and West Indies, married a Japanese—became a naturalized Japanese and a Buddhist, and changed his name to Yakumo Koizumi![9]

Hearn's life has often been called "unbelievable," as if it were the adventures of several people, or what Hearn himself called multiple personalities, some of whom he chose not to record. Granting that facts about a life can never be wholly accurate, we can develop the Ripley version with a few less exclamatory, if no less extraordinary, truths.

Hearn led, wrote Malcolm Cowley, the most exotic life of any nineteenth-century American author.[10] Yet this man of blurred citizenship, though he lived more years in America than in any other country, was not an American. Patrick Lafcadio (christened "Lefcadio") Tessima Carlos Hearn, his mother a Greek, his father a surgeon in the British army, carried English identification papers until the last years of his life. He was born in 1850 on the Greek island of Levkás, or Lefcadia—known to the British, who controlled it, as St. Maura. (Levkás is renowned as the island where the despairing Sappho threw herself down sea cliffs to her death.) On his father's side Hearn's Anglo-Irish family may originally have had Gypsy blood. His mother's relatives, with distant aristocratic connections and a high sense of family honor, were at least as exotic. They did not appreciate Charles Bush Hearn's attentions to Rosa Cassimati. Perhaps embellishing family history, Hearn himself wrote: "My father was attacked by my mother's brother, terribly stabbed, and left for dead. He recovered, and eloped with my mother."[11] Whatever the circumstances, the young medical officer became intimate with the woman, married her, then left her for several years when the army transferred him to the British West Indies.

At the age of two, Hearn traveled with his mother to Dublin, home of his father's family. At that time, like his mother, he spoke only Romaic. Now he learned a new language and had to adopt Patrick, or "Paddy," as his name for many years to come. Hearn stayed in Dublin after 1854, when his mother returned to her Greek island and his father went off to serve in the Crimea. Later, having contrived the dissolution of the marriage (probably by annulment), his father sailed with a new wife, a former sweetheart, to India; he died of a tropical disease in 1866 when returning home. Hearn's mother, who went insane in later years, married a man who refused to have children from a former marriage in his house, so Hearn was condemned to a loveless and lonely childhood. Evidently he could not forgive his father, whom he rarely mentioned, though he turned often and generously to thoughts about his mother. Writing during his Japan years to his half-sister, Minnie Atkinson, or creating his brilliant but fragmentary autobiographical accounts,[12] Hearn portrays his mother as someone of a special breed, a kind of maternal goddess smiling over his birthplace and early childhood. He also pays public tribute in *Out of the East: Reveries and Studies in New Japan* (1895):

All that country and time were softly ruled by One who thought only of ways to make me happy. Sometimes I would refuse to be made happy, and that always caused her pain. . . . She would tell me stories that made me tingle from head to foot with pleasure. I have never heard any other stories half so beautiful.[13]

However much issues of loss and abandonment dominate Hearn's books and private letters, he never so much as hints that his mother was forced to leave him as a child in a dark, rain-sodden city with unfeeling and unsympathetic relatives.

For the rest of his boyhood Hearn was supported by an aunt, Sarah Brenane, who, to the chagrin of her Anglican family, had married an Irish Catholic. She alone accepted responsibility for the boy while inflicting on him her fierce and prudish beliefs. When someone in her household drew crude pictures of clothing to mask the pubic areas in a book of Greek prints that "the Child" had discovered, Hearn's lifelong sense of mystery and longing were aroused. In his autobiographical sketches Hearn recalls a world like that of Charlotte Brontë's *Jane Eyre*, where, locked in unlit and silent rooms and terrified by his own "Cousin Jane," who told lurid accounts of hell and damnation, he had to endure appalling loneliness.[14] Notwithstanding occasional lip service to Catholic and Protestant churches in some of his newspaper articles, Hearn grew to hate any kind of Christianity. Nor did he, in the words of the "Believe It or Not" column, "become a Buddhist," albeit his praise of Shinto and Buddhist beliefs testifies to a welcome recognition of their distance from the strangling Christianity of his childhood.

Possibly because she could neither understand nor control her ward, Hearn's aunt sent him abroad to Catholic schools. He may have gone first to France and the dirty, oppressive school where his near contemporary, Guy de Maupassant, followed him as a student; Hearn never met Maupassant, whose stories he subsequently translated. He also attended St. Cuthbert's College at Ushaw, near Durham, in the North of England.[15] If not "raised in Wales," he spent summers there, as his autobiographical story "Hi-Mawari," from *Kwaidan: Stories and Studies of Strange Things* (1904) recalls.[16] Even as a child, this self-styled "nomad" rarely stayed long in one place, and the pattern, established first by others, continued by choice.

When still a small boy, Hearn said that he had slashed his knee with his father's sword and had been bedridden for months.[17] As a student of sixteen, he suffered another bizarre and more damaging accident. During a game, a piece of rope hit him in the face, blinding his left eye. Not only did this strain his other eye, which swelled and continued to give him pain; it also made him feel alien and grotesque—one cause, no doubt, of his chronic shyness and troubled relationships.

After his aunt lost her money to Henry Molyneux, a man who had swindled her (without losing her confidence), Hearn was placed in an ex-servant's house in London, from which he escaped to sleep in stables and to subsist in ways that he would remember with pain. In later years he described himself lying in the straw above well-fed and healthy horses, estimating how much he might be worth relative to the animals below.[18] Only incidental details of these and other months of misfortune are known. It is known that he was shipped off again, at the urging of Henry Molyneux, to Cincinnati, then the largest inland city in the United States and beset by all the imaginable social problems of growth and change.[19] Like a new Ben Franklin, he arrived without friends in the city and received only token help from the people to whom he had been sent. This was 1869; Hearn was nineteen.

In Japan many years afterward, Hearn offered one of his not uncommon apologies, this one to Basil Hall Chamberlain, effectively summing up his early privations and their unresolved legacies:

Let me venture to start out by confessing that I have never had any training to speak of. I had no home since a child, and no real schooling—never having graduated anywhere. Excepting elementary matters, I have taught myself the little I know. Then [in early years] I had to make headway against difficulties you could form no idea about (unless I should bore you by hinting of them), with nothing to guide me much better than instinct. After all, I have not made an utter failure of everything; but that kind of struggle leaves marks on a man, spoils his balance sometimes, and may even make him, at intervals, unconsciously offensive.[20]

Hearn's struggle in Cincinnati lasted many months. Suffering hunger and homelessness, he at last won the affection and help of an English printer, Henry Watkin, who, despite his own poverty, provided Hearn with shelter and the opportunity to find work. Until the last years of Watkin's life, Hearn continued to address him as "Dear Old Man" and "Dear Old Dad,"[21] acknowledging that Watkin had saved his life.

Moving through various odd jobs as salesman, printer, and copy editor, Hearn finally made his career as a journalist, reporting gruesome events and paralleling, in overwritten but powerful accounts, the yellow journalism and sensational popular novels of his age. He haunted the river wharves at night, explored the city's underworld and the black ghettos, described the last days and seconds of a man who was twice hanged, and actually made his fame when he recounted for his readers the then notorious Tanyard murder of a young man prodded by his lover's father and another man into a furnace in which he may have been burned alive.[22] Not all Hearn's writing focused on the gruesome; as Henry Mayhew had done earlier in his rendering of the London poor, he attended to pressing social issues, to the backgrounds of crime and poverty, to the sordid inner life of the city.[23] Through Hearn's writings for the *Enquirer* and later for the *Commercial*, Cincinnati readers vicariously experienced the worlds of indigents, criminals, con artists, prostitutes, immigrants, and ex-slaves.[24]

During his years of apprenticeship and horror reporting, Hearn spent much of his free time in the Cincinnati Public Library, reading widely in European literature, contemporary psychology, and science. If, as he says, his formal education amounted to little, he tried on his own to make up for its deficiency. He had not yet read Herbert Spencer, but he was in a sense preparing for the overarching system that Spencer would provide. Many of his writings, for example, dealt with technology and science, often with a morbid focus on such things as "Skulls and Skeletons," "Mad-House Horrors," or the "Dance of Death," the last an essay about dissecting rooms. His range of interests was astonishingly wide. Joining with the artist-illustrator, H. F. Farny, he founded a short-lived satirical magazine, *Ye Giglampz*, a reminder that at this stage in his career he still allowed wit and humor in his public writings. More successfully, he began his translations of contemporary French literature, including works by Théophile Gautier, Anatole France, Gustave Flaubert, and Maupassant. For a number of French authors, Hearn's were the first published English translations. (His translation of Maupassant's "A String of Pearls" still appears in anthologies.) He also reviewed new literary works, among them a story by the young and "first class word-painter" Henry James.[25] Immersed in the life of the city for his reporting, he found a few hours each day to educate himself in the literature and philosophy of his time.

Hearn's private life became more complicated than usual when he married Alethea (Mattie) Foley, a young woman talented, like his mother and his future wife in Japan, as a storyteller. She "possessed naturally a wonderful wealth of verbal description, a more than ordinarily vivid memory, and a gift of conversation which would have charmed an Italian *Improvisatore.*"[26] As Hearn evidently knew, their marriage had no legal standing. Technically a "Negro," Mattie was a fair-skinned woman who had been born a slave, and marriage between whites and blacks was in those years and in that region forbidden. Hearn complicated matters further by asking a black clergyman to perform the ceremony.

Later, in New Orleans and Martinique, Hearn speculated about racial differences and spoke of research into racial and ethnic characteristics in bodily types, temperament, and talent for fields such as music. He became fascinated by Creole and African-American women, many of whom he met (and paid) as prostitutes. Hearn often equated sexual excitement with racial difference, which meant, inevitably, differences in education and economic status. His wife herself slipped into the netherworld of Cincinnati, spurning Hearn's offers of help and insisting on her anonymity. "The lower she falls, the fonder I feel of her," Hearn wrote, unusually inattentive to issues of racial and sexist bigotry and apparently unaware of his self-disclosure.[27] Mattie, who survived these times and later claimed part of Hearn's estate, spoke more pointedly. "Nothing ever suited him," she said, any more than his "morose" temperament suited her.[28] The relationship proved painful for both Hearn and Mattie, and public disapproval when their marriage became known helped persuade him to leave Cincinnati in October 1877 for New Orleans.

Following another long period of near starvation Hearn once again became a successful journalist, reporting by preference the city's Creole past and customs and publishing (in 1885) a book on *La Cuisine Créole: A Collection of Culinary Recipes* and *"Gombo Zhèbes": A Little Dictionary of Creole Proverbs.*[29] He pursued his translations of contemporary French literature, which now appeared in print, and wrote what has been called America's first column for the New Orleans *Item,* a minor newspaper.[30] Covering topics as unlike as the shortcomings of Matthew Arnold and the opportunities for "Hot Baths in the Middle Ages," he produced another steady flow of articles.[31] The New Orleans years were exceptionally fruitful for Hearn, who, apart from his Creole books, began to publish new kinds of work, including his first novel. *Chita: A Memory of Last Island* (1889), a topographical and historical tour de force more than a narrative, pulled together from incidents associated with the 1856 destruction of Ile Dernière in the Gulf of Mexico (and Hearn's encounter with dengue fever), offers sensual evocations of the Gulf and the Louisiana bayous.[32]

In anticipation of his Japanese books Hearn also wrote pieces on Chinese and Japanese culture and on "inherited memory," a theory he had discovered in Herbert Spencer. Reading Spencer came almost as a revelation, if not as a conversion, since Spencer made possible a new vision of his past life and future work. He spoke at this time about Spencer supplanting all the vague "Oriental" thinking he had previously indulged in, unaware that he would come to credit Far Eastern, especially Buddhist, thought with tempering his response to Herbert Spencer.

In 1887, after ten years in the city, Hearn complained of being "weary of New Orleans."[33] Once more he wanted a new culture and a new landscape, which he found for a time in Martinique. Enchanted by St. Pierre, the town that in 1902 would be destroyed by Mount Pelée, the island's volcano, he fell in love with the tropics generally and explored as far away as the coast of Venezuela. Following his usual pattern, he endured months of hardship and a sporadic income. His private letters to a New Orleans friend, Dr. Rudolph Matas, admit to unattainable "chastity," fear of reinfection from venereal disease, a kind of abandon to a tropical world that made writing desultory, if not much of the time impossible.[34]

It was in Martinique that Hearn wrote his second and last piece of extended fiction, *Youma: The Story of a West-Indian Slave* (1890), another historical novel that captures the lush landscape of the island rather than the psychological complexity of its slave-woman character or the daily realities of her life.[35] The shortcomings of *Youma* forced Hearn to realize that his talents did not lie in novel writing. As usual, his rigorous self-criticism made weaknesses into larger signs of failure: "I have no *creative* talent, no constructive ability for the manufacture of fiction. I cannot write a story."[36] He could write fine *short* pieces, anecdotes and vignettes, but he could not, in his longer fiction, bring together his rigorous journalistic training with more self-conscious and evocative prose.

A work contemporary with *Youma*, *Two Years in the*

French West Indies (1890), offers a good indication of his chromatically and physically intense writing, along with disclaimers about haste and incompleteness, about notes, which characterize his piecemeal, or, as he described it, "impressionistic" method. Whether or not *Two Years* is the "masterpiece" it has been called, it illustrates the compelling and descriptive power of Hearn's "prose poetry."[37] His recorded journey from New York to the Caribbean has many of the qualities that, refined by the experience in Japan, emerge in *Glimpses of Unfamiliar Japan* (1894), Hearn's first book-length account of that country.[38] What he seemed to be seeking and manifestly found in his later books was a way of focusing his writing on his own ways of looking, transposing fragments of the world he saw into subtle parts of a larger, if never fully articulated, whole.

Hearn remained in Martinique from October 1887 until May 1889. His departure, like the later departure from Matsue, Japan, was painful: "It seemed like tearing my heart out to leave Martinique."[39]

For a few weeks after his stay in Martinique, Hearn went to Philadelphia to live in the house of the eye specialist, George Gould, with whom he had already corresponded from New Orleans. Hearn's friendship with Gould offers a paradigm for his male relationships: It began with mutual respect and Hearn's adulation of this man of "science," who played the role of self-confident mentor—ambitious and disciplined, with "well-developed ideas of order and system."[40] Confiding in Gould as he had in Matas, another medical doctor, he spoke of his aspirations, literary projects, and sexual frustrations, admitting to personal and professional failures, except that with Gould the relationship deteriorated upon closer acquaintance, putting an end to the awkward intimacy of "Hearney boy" and "Gooldey" attempted in Hearn's letters. When he moved into Gould's house and learned more about the man he had unquestioningly trusted, he became skeptical, just as Gould became patronizing. Soon open misunderstandings developed, early affection turned to dislike, and Hearn,

feeling mistreated and betrayed, left in disgust. Later con-
fiscating Hearn's book collection, Gould also wrote his
vituperative attacks on Hearn's character and creative
powers and devoted much of his energy to making cruel,
even though at times accurate, assessments.[41]

After Philadelphia Hearn returned to New York, where
he had stopped reluctantly several times before. In New
York lived a former Cincinnati friend, the musicologist
Henry E. Krehbiel, who now seemed to keep his distance.
No doubt more disconcerting, Hearn saw little of Elizabeth Bisland, a young writer he had met in New Orleans
and who, as his letters over the years reveal, represented
the women he needed to worship from a distance. Confessing before his departure for Japan that his friendship was
something closer to love, Hearn evidently never managed
to mix his sexual passions with his idolizing of independent or socially advantaged women.[42] On the whole, he
remained careful, if not quite laconic, when speaking of
Bisland to friends: "I met Miss Bisland again," he confided
to Matas. "She had expanded mentally and physically into
one of the most superb women you could wish to converse
with."[43]

Bisland appreciated Hearn, praising him unreservedly in
her 1906 study, *Lafcadio Hearn: Life and Letters.* "A more
delightful or—at times—more fantastically witty companion it would be impossible to imagine, but it is equally
impossible to attempt to convey his astounding sensitive-
ness."[44] Hearn's wit, apparent in his numerous drawings
and in the uncensored idiom of private letters, comes and
goes with his moods; his shyness was more consistent.
Whether from a conviction of his own failings or a need for
unconditional approval, his shyness kept him separate
from Bisland and others he admired. Not only did he need
to be trapped into a dinner engagement, a meeting with
fellow writers, or any sort of social event, he would also run
away while waiting at a door or disappear when meeting
unexpected people. Fortunately, a new friend, the chemical
engineer Ellwood Hendrick, allowed him easy and cordial

relations, making New York a little more tolerable. Quite apart from his shyness, he hated New York, which he later contrasted as a diabolical machine with the village quality of Tokyo. In truth he hated any large city, Tokyo included.

2   There is scarcely another man in history who has become . . . a sympathetic symbol to two different cultures.

               —Earl Miner, *The Japanese Tradition in British and American Literature*

At the instigation of William Patten, an art editor with *Harper's Magazine,* the president of Canadian Pacific Railway offered Hearn free transportation to Japan, insisting only that he write about his experiences. This was in the spring of 1890. The invitation led to a welcome escape from New York and in a sense to the culmination of a long process of thinking about Japan. Hearn had speculated in New Orleans about "a secret law of force compelling all intelligent life to flow . . . from West to East," from Europe and America, in other words, to the Orient.[45] Through Ichizo Hattori, the Japanese representative in charge of the Japanese section of the New Orleans World Exposition (1884–85), he had become intrigued by Japan and its social and cultural identity. In fact, Hattori and the exposition fed his growing appetite about Oriental topics, which manifested itself in articles on Japanese poetry, translations of Japanese impressions by Pierre Loti, and long studies of Buddhism.

After Martinique, Japan had tempted him as a possible next destination. Encouraged by friends and newly inspired by Percival Lowell's *The Soul of the Far East,* published in 1888, he had already contemplated a study of Japan:

In attempting a book upon a country so well trodden as Japan, I could not hope—nor would I consider it prudent attempting,—to discover totally new things, but to create, in the minds of the readers, a vivid impression of *living* in Japan,—not simply as an observer but as one taking part in the daily existence of the common people, and *thinking with their thoughts*.[46]

Except that Hearn grew to acknowledge the futility of entering the lives and thoughts of Japanese people, the prospectus identifies exactly the ambitions of his future books.

Sometimes he spoke of the journey as an opportunity, sometimes as a necessity. His travels, described for a *Harper's* article, never appeared among the first impressions given in *Glimpses of Unfamiliar Japan*, which begins with the sketch "My First Day in the Orient." Hearn records his train journey across frozen Canada and sixteen days on the steamship *Abyssinia*, ending with his arrival and the recognition that "I am in Japan."[47] Most early commentators emphasized the excitement of approach— the slowly developing vistas, the first signs of the new land—whereas Hearn begins his book with the whirlwind sensations of being there.

The "Winter Journey to Japan" recalls Hearn's article of 1879, "Travel, an Educating Influence," in which he had written that America was "the least cosmopolitan nation in the world." Only recently could it "boast a few travellers who really know how to travel."[48] With his diffidence and sense of awkwardness, Hearn himself hardly seems cosmopolitan. He did know how to travel, and his essay for *Harper's* proved the first installment of a long and unmatched travel report.

As for many Westerners, Hearn's journey to Japan meant coming home, both a return—as Goethe had written—to "the origins of the human race" and a fulfillment of vague and exalted desires.[49] For Hearn personally, return went beyond romantic cliché to a profound conviction of his own origins, in a place that touched the Orient and reached backward in time. "How marvelously," he says, "does this world resemble antique Greece,—not merely in its legends and the more joyous phases of its faith, but in all its graces of art and its senses of beauty."[50] Like his contemporary, the Anglo-Irish novelist George Moore, he associated Greek "paganism" with beauty, which for both men was a remembered beauty, not a cognition, in words they both used, but a *recognition*.

Distant though it was from his birthplace, Japan spoke to him of things he knew. In *Out of the East* he writes of a kind of déjà vu that flashes on his mind when telling a Japanese folktale: "I have a memory of a place and a magical time in which the Sun and the Moon were larger and brighter than now. Whether it was of this life or of some life before I cannot tell. But I know the sky was very much more blue, and nearer to the world."[51]

Hearn was prepared to make Japan a magical land, which meant once again the land of his remembering. "He used to say," according to his second wife, Setsuko (or Setsu) Koizumi, "that he was born Japanese, and accidentally [appeared] in the wrong place . . . but finally found his own home and returned to Japan."[52] He sought a kind of utopia and, for a time, managed to realize it; and if, as Herbert Marcuse has written, all utopian thinking is "grounded in recollection" (a view to which Hearn would have subscribed),[53] Lafcadio Hearn's utopia recalled an older, more satisfying civilization. This was a Japan of his own making and at the same time a briefly felt return to the world of his mother and his childhood.

Once in Japan, Hearn's new beginnings led to the now predictable dislocations, economic as well as personal. Raptures aside, he sometimes regretted his decision, missing the tropical Caribbean or fretting about his circumstances:

It was a bad business for me, this trip to Japan. First, the artist, who is an ignorant brute and unbearably disagreeable, went back on his word to make the first payment from the C[anadian] P[acific] R.R. over to me. Secondly, I found rates of living higher in Yokohama than New York. Thirdly, the conditions of the Harpers rendered living by literary work wholly out of the possible. Fourthly, I could not get out of Japan. Fifthly, I could not get employment.

He adds, in deeper despair: "It seems to me for the first time that my life is really a failure."[54] Not for the first time, he ensured that things got worse. Dashing off insulting letters to Henry Alden, editor of *Harper's*, and cutting Weldon, the illustrator who controlled the small expense monies available to him in Yokohama (and who had, to Hearn's chagrin, been promised twice his own stipend), Hearn made return to either the United States or the tropics temporarily impossible. He now drew on new friends, especially Mitchell McDonald, paymaster of the United States Navy, a man who managed to retain his friendship, and Basil Hall Chamberlain, a loyal and less fortunate supporter.[55]

If, as one Japanese contemporary put it, Chamberlain was to Hearn "not his helper but his great teacher,"[56] introducing him to literature about Japan and sharing his vast knowledge about the country's history, their correspondence shows each learning and benefiting from mutual support, even when Hearn writes to his friend with the overstated deference with which he had flattered George Gould. Chamberlain understood Hearn far better than Hearn understood him, and he sympathized with Hearn's decision to end their friendship, despite the irony that the two came at last to live in the same city.[57] Whether antagonistic like Gould or supportive like Chamberlain, few people escaped Hearn's pattern of friendship, which moved predictably from a kind of adulation to irritation or even bitterness and ended with Hearn's pointed silence. Hearn insisted that the great gains in his life resulted from "disillusion" rather than from friends.[58] Some of his disillusion must have come from his treatment of friends.

No less than Hearn an apologist for Japan, Chamberlain had two qualities regrettably lacking in Hearn: the consistent grace of good humor and a reluctance to embellish.[59] His pioneering study, *Things Japanese: Being Notes on Various Subjects Connected with Japan,* published in 1890, cites Hearn in later editions, although Chamberlain made less complimentary remarks after Hearn's death, and he sometimes complained about Hearn's overwrought prose. Anticipating recent rejections of a vague Orientalism, Chamberlain also pointed out the folly of loose associations between countries thousands of miles apart. Hearn entertained no such misgivings. If he wanted to imagine Japan and Greece as part of a historic continuum or in metaphoric relationship, he would do so.

It was Chamberlain who guided Hearn toward a job—as a teacher rather than a journalist—enlisting the help of Ichizo Hattori, the man Hearn met at the New Orleans exposition. Hearn had arrived in Japan at a time when the Meiji government still honored and sought out Western teachers. Chamberlain himself had become an esteemed professor of Japanese at Tokyo Imperial University, one of a number of foreigners teaching in higher education. On short notice, Chamberlain could find no attractive opportunity for Hearn, who finally accepted a lower-level teaching position in Matsue, Shimane prefecture, the prospect of which must have seemed like banishment to a remote part of the empire. Unsure of his abilities, untrained for the work, and having little choice, Hearn left in the summer of 1890 for his new professional assignment.

As he describes it in *Glimpses*, Hearn's trek to Matsue, on the Sea of Japan coast, grew into an experience of profound discovery. He makes no mention of the train ride from Tokyo to the end of the line in Okayama;[60] the journey began for him when, leaving trains and the mechanical world behind, he wound slowly over mountains through rural Japan. Apart from its remoteness, Matsue seemed to him, as tradition enshrined it to the Japanese, a holy setting. He entitled a major section of *Glimpses* "The Chief City of the Province of the Gods," and he quickly felt comfortable with its people as well as its gods. (Hearn always spoke of the province as Izumo, but Matsue was now the capital city of Shimane prefecture, a part of the old province.)

The prefectural governor befriended him, as did Nishida Sentarō, principal of the school where he taught and, until his death in 1898, one of Hearn's closest Japanese friends. People greeted him on the streets as if he were a distinguished visitor, and he was apparently just the third Westerner to reside in Matsue. Here he mixed with others of his own stature, with whom his odd appearance was either taken for granted—who knew, after all, what barbarians *should* look like?—or remained a matter for courteous disregard.[61] Only in retrospect did he realize that his perceptions may have been self-flattering. His friend Nishida disabused him of illusions that he had been loved in Matsue or that the city represented a particularly friendly part of Japan. Not so, Nishida wrote, in an effort to make Hearn's new life less troubling. Although people in Matsue had been attentive, it would be a mistake to think them more friendly than curious. By claiming that people elsewhere in Japan showed less civility, he overlooked the provincial nature of Matsue, a town as yet unused to foreigners.[62]

Despite Nishida's deflating remarks and a stay of only fifteen months, Matsue defined for Hearn what Japan had been and should have remained. A small castle town presided over by the "little Fuji," Mount Daisen, Matsue lay elegantly on the shore of Lake Shinji, which connects with the Sea of Japan. More than a place in Hearn's mind, it represented the best of ancient values operating in a world that was no longer feudal (if that is an appropriate word for pre-Meiji Japan) nor running pell-mell after Western models.

Writing in *Glimpses* about his wrenching departure from Matsue, Hearn slips into present tense, as if to live again the intensity of the experience.

Magical indeed the charm of this land, as of a land veritably haunted by gods: so lovely the spectral delicacy of its colors,—so lovely the forms of its hills blending with the forms of its clouds,—so lovely, above all, those long trailings and bandings of mists which make its altitudes appear to hang in air. A land where sky and earth so strangely intermingle that what is reality may not be distinguished from what is illusion,—that all seems a mirage, about to vanish. For me, alas! it is about to vanish forever.

It does vanish. When the small ship pulls away, taking him "more and more swiftly, ever farther and farther from the Province of the Gods,"[63] Hearn speaks of "my heart" and "my home," implying that he left as he had come, unattached. He had in fact married in Matsue. During an illness caused by the protracted cold of the winter, he had become dangerously ill, and Setsu Koizumi, twenty-two-year-old daughter of an impoverished samurai family, nursed him back to health.[64] Most marriages between Western men and Japanese women involved a sort of acceptable concubinage, frowned upon by Japanese authorities, unrecognized by Western governments. Although repeating in form his legally dubious marriage to Mattie Foley, Hearn took the new relationship seriously. Marrying Setsu, he married her family, or at least accepted financial responsibility for her immediate relatives. Why then do so few of the public writings allude to his marriage or to his wife as companion? Apart from mentioning a guide or describing the individuals he meets, he writes as if he remained alone throughout the years in Japan. And in a certain sense this is true. Hearn unquestionably both admired and kept a certain distance from his "little" wife, whereas she admitted that in Matsue, if not elsewhere, she had thought him crazy beyond the unpredictability of his foreignness.

Setsu, like Mattie Foley before her, provided Hearn with material for his writing—along with a key to the Japanese language. Unable to translate Japanese, he would ask his wife to retell stories in *her* way, praising her lack of literary skills or imperfect knowledge, then render her tales into his own distinctive style. Because neither mastered the other's language, they apparently spoke in a kind of primitive Japanese, inventing their means of discourse. But these ambivalences aside, Hearn's process of immersing himself in a spoken story, recapturing his early childhood when a gentle woman read to him about a magical world, testifies to his lifelong need for comfort and maternal care. His own word for this was always *sympathy*.

After leaving Matsue, Hearn transferred to another teaching job in the larger and less attractive city of Kumamoto on the island of Kyushu, a place he never came to love. Here he felt isolated and rejected, unwelcomed by the other teachers and lonely without his Izumo friends. He was soon writing to Chamberlain and their acquaintance, W. B. Mason, asking for help. Then in 1896, without his friends' intervention, he secured a journalism position with the Kobe *Chronicle*, a newspaper devoted to Western life in the treaty port, though sympathetic on balance to the Japanese. Its editor, a Scot named Robert Young, treated Hearn hospitably and invited his writing of editorials. Unfortunately, return to daily journalism strained Hearn's eyesight so badly he was forced to remain for weeks in a darkened room—and to think about other means of earning a living. Thanks finally to Chamberlain's help, he was offered the post of lecturer in English at the Imperial University in Tokyo, where he taught for the next six years. New circumstances dictated that he could not be a "professor," the title reserved for "foreign" teachers.

For not only had Hearn married Setsu Koizumi, he had also—to protect his wife's legal rights—taken Japanese citizenship himself. He became and often signed himself Koizumi Yakumo, "or—arranging the personal and family names in English order—'Y. Koizumi.'" As his self-romanticizing etymology suggests, Yakumo, drawn from the oldest known Japanese poem, "is a poetical alternative for Izumo, my beloved province, 'the Place of the Issuing of Clouds.' You will understand how the name was chosen."[65] This unusual and, to the Japanese, unwelcome "conversion," which credits Hearn's generosity to his family, points once more to his lifetime readiness for change. The Greek island boy, who had become Patrick and Paddy, then Lafcadio, accepted a new identity as a sign, if not of becoming Japanese, which he acknowledged to be impossible, then at least of commitment to his life in Japan. The Japanese, who have honored Hearn's memory with festivals, museums, and extensive scholarly activity, refer to him as Koizumi Yakumo—and rightly, since he enjoyed using the name with Japanese acquaintances.

Hearn had complained of ill health for some time, and doubtless the effects of stress, early malnutrition, repeated illnesses, and unstinting hard work must have taken their toll. He died of hear failure on 26 September 1904. He was fifty-four years old.

3   The years, after all, have a kind of emptiness when we spend too many of them on a foreign shore. We defer the reality of life, in such cases, until a *future* moment when we shall again breathe our *native air;* but, by and by, there are no *future* moments; or, if we do return, we find that life has shifted its reality to the spot where we have deemed ourselves only temporary residents. Thus, between two *countries,* we have none at all, or only that little space of either in which we finally lay down our discontented bones.
            —Nathaniel Hawthorne, *The Marble Faun; or,*
                                The Romance of Monte Beni

Probably no country has changed more than Japan in the hundred years since Lafcadio Hearn landed in Yokohama. Not many had changed so dramatically in the years before his landing. Surprisingly, for a few years after the arrival of Commodore Perry's "Black Ships" in 1853 and 1854, Western relations with Japan remained limited. Townsend Harris's treaty of 1858 hastened the radical changes. First, the treaty ports were established, mainly in the 1860s, which allowed for commerce and restricted Western access. Ironically, one powerful force behind the 1868 revolution involved dissatisfaction with foreign meddling, yet the reforming samurai themselves opted for Westernization, insisting on the need for Western might in order to compete with Western nations. It was they, not the failing Tokugawa shogunate, who invited Western trade, technology, and teachers.

By the time of Hearn's arrival, Japan had transformed itself from an isolationist and technologically undeveloped country to an industrial and military power, eager to Westernize and determined to prevail. In 1882 one of the new leaders, Ito Hirobumi (formerly a samurai from the Choshu region), had traveled to Europe to study Western constitutions,[66] and, while Japan borrowed its rail and naval models from Great Britain, it looked for a less democratic political system in Germany.[67] Following elections of July 1890, a few months after Hearn's arrival, Japan's first constitutional government was soon sitting, acrimoniously, in Tokyo.

In obvious ways the country in which Hearn came to live underwent radical metamorphosis, democratizing to a minimal extent, with a tiny electorate, while elevating the emperor as the symbol of the country's military growth. *Fukoku-kyohei,* "a rich country with a strong army," had been one slogan of the reforming samurai; *sonno-joi,* "honor the emperor, expel the barbarian," was another. By 1894 Hearn's own students were to die in the war with China, and Hearn himself died the year Japanese ships captured Port Arthur (now Lüshun) to begin the first rout in modern history of a (self-styled) European by an Asian country. As with the Europeans themselves, military power stimulated colonial ambitions, and, conversely, those ambitions drove Japan to military development. Late editions of *Handbook for Travellers,* by B. H. Chamberlain and W. B. Mason, included the recently subjugated Formosa (now Taiwan) as an extension of Japan.[68] In 1910 Chosen (Korea) became another colony. Manchuria would follow. Though shrewdly perceptive about the domestic implications of industrial and military growth, Hearn never appreciated the connection between Japan's nationalism and its empire building.[69]

The history of Japan in the years before and after the Meiji restoration is, as G. B. Sansom shows, complicated, and the role of Westerners, changing over the years, must have been continually puzzling to the men and women who had chosen to live in Japan.[70] Many were at first welcomed, only to be pushed aside in later years; many never accepted their role or status in a society disturbingly remote from what they had previously known. Few mastered the language. As the building of railroads advanced, Westerners gained access to remoter parts of the country, what they called, like their counterparts elsewhere, "the interior," and greater familiarity raised doubts and questions. Increasingly, studies of Japan after the 1850s spoke of enigma and contradiction,[71] and while writers like Chamberlain or William G. Aston shed light on a long history and complex social structures, the spate of inquiring books testified to the difficulties inherent in Western knowledge about the country.

From the outset, Hearn wisely recognized his own limitations. He avoided pronouncements and simple generalizations, his habit of "impressionism" prompting the open responsiveness necessary for genuine insight. Like any visitor, of course, he saw only scattered segments of the country. Yet over the years, whether in published essays for the *Atlantic Monthly* or in talks to students or in articles for the Kobe *Chronicle*, Hearn touched on an unprecedented wealth of topics and used his impressions as a way to address subtle issues of Japanese civilization. Part of the complexity, and the appeal, of Hearn's writings comes from his wrestling with such issues, which alter his vision of Japan and undercut his early infatuation. The mature vision, not without enormous personal cost, resulted in rich and insightful books.

It might be said that Hearn lived increasingly less in Japan the longer he stayed. When, for example, he and his family moved to their last house in Tokyo, he had nothing to do with its planning or supervision, except to say that he wanted a quiet place to work and, because he suffered from the cold, a stove in his room. After an early visit, he left the arrangements to his wife. "I know how to write," he said, "and that is all."[72] Certainly that was all he wanted—and wanted with increasing urgency. Like another self-conscious exile, Henry James, he sought the safety and the challenge of his four brown walls, his writing almost a substitute for physical living.

Paradoxically, Hearn's retreat to his writing desk provided, in his wife's words, another "return to Japan," a means of ensuring his continued residence, which in part he evidently wanted: "The Japanese are still the best people in the world to live among; and therefore why wish ever to live elsewhere?"[73] Hearn insisted whenever possible on dressing like the Japanese and honoring Japanese traditions, though he soon lost enthusiasm for Japanese food. "He always wanted to live," according to his wife, "in the midst of purely Japanese surroundings."[74] In another country compatriots would have charged him with "going native," with a renunciation of his own kind. For Hearn the renunciation was both illusory and real. It meant finally a renunciation of past and present life, a reduction of experience that allowed for a monastic concentration on what he held most dear.

4   Homesickness was a luxury I remember craving from the tenderest age.
    —Henry James, letter of 28 July 1883

I want to touch on questions of home and exile in another way, beginning with the observation that Hearn was an outstanding swimmer. In *Glimpses* and other writings he speaks of a compulsion to jump, often at night, out of boats or even hotel windows into any kind of water. The one known time he contemplated suicide, he thought of drowning—an odd notion for someone who prided himself on swimming as his only physical skill.[75] Whether in Izumo or, in his last years, at Yaezu, he would swim out through high surf, well beyond the area where most bathers felt safe, unconcerned about treacherous tides or currents. Japanese innkeepers and Hearn's friends wondered about the man who dropped clothes and money, everything that could be left behind, unattended on the shore. Proud of his abilities, he thought of himself as unsinkable. An image of this ungainly man perfectly at ease in the wide sea, far from the possibility of rescue, points to a defining condition of Hearn's exile, the sense that he had of Karma, of larger forces shaping his life.[76]

Among Japanese legends he preferred that of the young fisherman, Urashima, who sails away from home and, because of an act of kindness, wins the love of the daughter of the god of the sea. For an illusively short time, he lives contentedly with his beautiful wife in what becomes his native element.[77]

Each day for Urashima there were new wonders and new pleasures:—wonders of the deepest deep brought up by the servants of the Ocean God;—pleasures of that enchanted land where summer never dies. And so three years passed.[78]

The quintessential exile, Urashima imagines himself in an apparently timeless world, far from the sufferings of ordinary mortals, enjoying what Hearn elsewhere calls "the silence of the great water."[79] He is the analogue of Matthew Arnold's mermaid and the many Western myths of escape and separation, love and betrayal; he also experiences what Sigmund Freud was to describe (with skepticism) as the feeling closest to "a sensation of 'eternity,' a feeling as of something limitless, unbounded," a basic religious condition.[80] That "oceanic" sensation has, to borrow Freud's term, corresponding "discontents," or, in the words Hearn finds for Urashima, "a heaviness at his heart," which applies pointedly to the author himself. Urashima learns the consequences of discontent after insisting on a return to his old homeland, where he suffers both separation from his ocean bride and his own dissolution. Heartbroken on his return to find his family long dead and unable to resist his wife's importunate warnings not to open a box she has given him, he loses everything:

Urashima then knew that he had destroyed his own happiness, that he could never again return to his beloved, the daughter of the Ocean King. So that he wept and cried out bitterly in his despair. . . . Yet for a moment only. In another, he himself was changed. An icy chill shot through all his blood;—his teeth fell out; his face shrivelled; his hair turned white as snow; his limbs withered; his strength ebbed; he sank down lifeless on the sand, crushed by the weight of four hundred winters.[81]

Hearn's own growing sense of isolation and dissolution weighed on him, if not already in Matsue then soon thereafter. He even pictured himself as Urashima. On returning to Izumo late in his life, he attended a folk dance:

At my request, the girl danced the dance of Urashima. I asked her because I had seen her dance it when she was a child. This time she danced it using a mask;—the mask of old age,—deftly slipped it on at the moment when Urashima looks into the box which he was told never to open. Afterwards she brought me the mask to look at. I thought that its pasteboard features had a faint mocking resemblance to my own.[82]

Hearn wrote to Mason in 1892 about "the utter isolation" of his Japanese exile,[83] and, in fact, this advocate for Japan, this lover of things Japanese, often bemoaned his exile and longed, with Urashima's "heaviness of heart," for something lost. That something was usually a smile or a voice or another epiphanic reminder of the past. Much of the time it centered on place. In Kumamoto, the "most uninteresting city I was ever in,"[84] he could say that he "must try to get into this exiled Western life [in the treaty ports], and love it and study it,—and tell all the beautiful things there are in it." And elsewhere: "Yes, I'm afraid one *could* be happy in the open ports. . . . They are the most beautiful cities in Japan. Kobe!—what a flood of light, with the amethyst hills massing into it."[85]

Settled in Kobe and complaining about the boorish and tasteless Westerners there, he wanted once more to return to Matsue and Izumo or to think about Tokyo. Although he chastised Chamberlain and Mason for failing to secure him a job in Tokyo, he had told them categorically of his distaste for the capital, a constant refrain when he lived there. "That troubled sea" of officialdom, which destroyed historic civility and blighted Japanese culture, made his own life impossible. No more so, however, than the ill-mannered new breed of Japanese or, at times, the entire population. Just as to Japanese friends he spoke of other Westerners as unpleasant, if not repulsive, so after a few years in Japan—and writing to fellow Westerners—he could say "I hate the Japanese" and "D___ Japan."[86] Sometimes Hearn's dissatisfaction took the form of anger, sometimes frustration, sometimes just a sad regret. He could write after several years in the country: "The beautiful illusion of Japan, the almost weird charm that comes with one's first entrance into her magical atmosphere, had, indeed, stayed with me very long, but had totally faded at last."[87]

His acknowledgement of the fading magic comes through more strongly in personal letters, in which Hearn admits to despair, to a sense of hopelessness scarcely remediable by affection for his adopted country. He spoke about leaving Japan, even at times that he might go without his family, though insisting that such a trip would benefit his family. A planned lecture series at the invitation of Cornell University—canceled because of a flu epidemic on campus—promised him a chance to return to America, to educate Kazuo, his eldest son, and possibly to escape Japan. Seeing Elizabeth Bisland, as his letters suggest, may also have been high on his list of reasons for entertaining the Cornell offer. To this woman he had long admired, Hearn wrote as a coy lover, commenting on how much his son would like to meet her and how prominently her picture stood in his "little" house where his "little" wife also paid homage to the distant and beautiful American woman. Unable to carry on a close relationship with Bisland in New Orleans or New York, Hearn created an ideal relationship from the Far East. Bisland aside, Hearn at fifty was probably homesick for Western people and Western things. He relished his meetings with Mitchell McDonald, who, as a naval officer and later a hotel owner, maintained in Yokohama a life unashamedly Western—as well as unacademic, unpretentious, and undemanding for a visitor like Hearn.

It would be impossible to say whether, given the right circumstances—and Hearn's lifelong inclination for change and uprooting—he might have left Japan as he left Martinique or New Orleans once the initial delight had paled. Certainly in Japan he moved from city to city and house to house. Now more than ever, financial considerations must have guided some of his thinking. "I would not stay in Japan another day," he said at one point, "but that I have a family to take care of."[88] In an 1892 letter to Mason he wrote: "I have just read that most frightful book by Kipling, 'The Light that Failed,' where he speaks of the horror of being in London without any money. Nobody can even dimly imagine . . . what the horror is, if he has not been there. And I have—in London, Cincinnati, New York, Memphis, New Orleans, Savannah,—not to speak of other places. . . . You never can get used to it."[89]

Japan provided Hearn with the comfort of adequate money and the opportunity for almost total independence. These in turn allowed him a kind of weightless exile, an exile within the larger exile of a changing Japan, free from responsibilities or obligation beyond the absolutely necessary. Unlike Urashima, and perhaps with Urashima's fate in mind, he did not choose to "go home" but, instead, wrote prolifically in what he admitted to be profound isolation. "Only by thus isolating himself," as he said of Tennyson, "could he have found time to accomplish the work he did."[90] Apart from the hours he spent alone writing, he seems to have been at his happiest when he could swim, day or night, out into the ocean, losing himself like the legendary fisherman.

[2]
Western Writers in Japan

1   I suppose you must know, or feel, that any one who
     wishes to be purely *himself*, must be isolated in all
     countries.
                                              —Lafcadio Hearn

Many Westerners had come to Japan before Lafcadio
Hearn—engineers and traders, sightseers and doctors, art
collectors and students of language. Photographers such as
Felice Beato and his successor Baron von Stillfried had recorded peasants and aristocrats from an older Japan, some
of whom still thought of photography as a theft of the soul.
And, of course, there were writers, legions of writers. Basil
Hall Chamberlain, speaking in *Things Japanese* about
"books on Japan," recommends works by Algernon B. Mitford, William G. Aston, Rutherford Alcock, Sir Ernest Sat-
ow, and their distinguished peers before offering a long list
of "others": "Where one has hundreds of books to choose
from, such a list . . . might be indefinitely extended. . . .
There is literally no end to the making of them." Responding generously to much of the work of his predecessors and
rivals, Chamberlain makes fun of books reflecting "every
possible space of time, from *Seven Weeks in Japan* to *Eight
Years in Japan*," or announcing themselves with allitera-
tive titles (*A Jaunt in Japan* and *Japanese Jingles*) or using
sundry "piquant" adjectives, from "the real Japan" to the
"heroic," the "ceremonial," the "practical," and the "pic-
turesque."[1]
    Above all, it was the picturesque that appealed to West-
ern audiences, the accounts of a strange and seductive land
filled with mysterious beauty and weird sounds, the Japan

31

of Sir Edwin Arnold and Lawrence Oliphant, who insisted on all that was exquisite and different. Chamberlain recorded the disappointment of a Japanese audience hearing Arnold's praise of the exotic beauty of traditional Japan.[2] If it was not, as Chamberlain said, what the Japanese hoped to hear, it was precisely what Arnold and other sympathetic visitors expected and saw.

To many interested Americans and Europeans in the years after the opening of the ports Japan remained both exotic and seductive. Painters from Toulouse-Lautrec to Gauguin used Japanese themes in their work, while Pierre Bonnard was to win from friends the facetious title of "the very Japanese Bonnard."[3] From household designs to clothing, the taste for Japanese fairy tales and legends, quaint costumes, and delicate ceremonies was almost epidemic. Both Gilbert and Sullivan's *The Mikado* and Puccini's *Madama Butterfly* testify to the fascinated reduction of Japan in the eyes of Westerners, who borrowed immense amounts of *Japonisme* and overlooked the lived reality or political and social conditions of the changing country.[4] This might have been, as Edward Said argues, inevitable for Westerners in the "Orient," who were intent on a world of their own realizing, the result of idyllic longings and a predictably selective "style of thought."[5] Yet perceptions of Japan always set it apart from the rest of the Orient, which Westerners perceived to be politically, economically, and militarily weak. They could admire the allure of Japan without despising it as a country. Whether or not this means that "nobody was ever patronizing about Japan,"[6] it does make more interesting the lasting contrasts between the appeal of an Oriental fairyland and "the enigma of Japanese power," itself a reflection of a robust if puzzling nation-state.[7]

To some extent, Hearn himself drew on the popular and aestheticized myth of Japan while creating his own necessary idyll. Long before he went to Japan, however, his selective but shrewd insights encompassed contradictory elements. Hearn had extolled Japanese arts and crafts in the

New Orleans World Industrial Exposition of 1884–85, and already by that time his interests tended to go deeper than those of his peers; they included the historical richness of the country, the complex local realities, the implications of the wisdom of Buddhism. As his early "The Soul of the Great Bell" (Chinese rather than Japanese) suggests, Hearn relished contradictions. In that story the casting of a bell fails to marry disparate parts, "for the metals had rebelled one against the other,—the gold had scorned alliance with the brass, the silver would not mingle with the molten iron."[8]

From the time of the New Orleans exposition, Hearn vacillated between praise for Japan's growing powers, the respect for force he found justified in Herbert Spencer, and his fears about modern industry, which he deplored in the West.[9] "Never," he had written about industrial force at the exposition, "did the might of machinery seem to me so awful. . . . I found myself still dreaming of that future cycle of centuries wherein the world's labors shall be performed by automatons."[10] The decline of craftsmanship in the West was something he worried about and anticipated for Japan, where handmade products were still everywhere available and factories remained satisfactorily small. Much as he came to admire Japan as a developing rival of Western countries (and was unusual in arguing this case), it was the "old Japan" that enticed him, the modern Japan that—in spite of his better judgment—repelled.

Professor Chamberlain spoke to me about the variability of one's feeling toward Japan being like the oscillation of a pendulum: one day swinging toward pessimism and the next to optimism. I have this feeling very often. But the pessimistic feeling is generally coincident with some experience of new Japan, & the optimistic with something of old Japan.[11]

Although in editorials for the Kobe *Chronicle* and in most of his books he dealt in passing with current political issues and social conditions, Hearn preferred topics that spoke to individual exploration, as if he were the treasure hunter and Japan his hidden cave. The metaphor is apt because he sought out caves and cavelike spaces, as, for example, the interiors of shrines, which hinted at mystery along with sanctuary. If all this constituted the "real" Japan as much as the industrialization of Yokohama, it proved a diminishing part, as Hearn quickly recognized. Aware of alternatives, he made his choice, and the man who had scoured Cincinnati for evidence of the gruesome wrote about Japan as if Japanese society had scarcely any nasty underside or he no appetite to assess it. This is not to say that he had lost his taste for horror or the grotesque, and certainly his youthful obsessions found muted forms in the Japanese writings, conspicuously in his pursuit of "ghostly" stories.

Just as there were in the eyes of most foreigners at least two Japans, the old and the new, the exotic and the practical, there were also three basic groups of visitors: those who came out of curiosity, whether scholars or "tourists" (that odd breed of travelers born and baptized in the nineteenth century);[12] those who attended, with and without the invitation of the Japanese, to matters of business, among them teachers like Hearn; and those who served as representatives of Western churches, the missionaries whom Lafcadio Hearn held in contempt. Often the last two groups overlapped, for the missionaries provided much of the instruction in English—and in other fields too, as a book such as *Clara's Diary* suggests. Published for the first time in 1979, Clara A. N. Whitney's candid entries record the struggles of one missionary family, whose members generously taught economics or English to the Japanese they met and remained dedicated to the conversion of "heathen."[13]

In Hearn's view, the missionaries were dangerous corrupters of Japan, meddlers who inflicted suffering on their converts, because they lacked all sense of the value of Eastern life, spiritual or day-to-day. Throughout the Kobe *Chronicle* articles and his books on Japan, he pokes repeatedly at the missionaries, relishing their counterattacks on him. He calls them cruel as well as foolish, his remarks as caustic as those of Somerset Maugham in a later generation. "Unconsciously, every honest being in the mission-army is a destroyer . . . for nothing can replace what they break down."[14] The apparently factual "Case of O Dai" tells of a young woman converted and mistreated by two Western missionaries, who finally cast her out and force her to become a prostitute. Christianity, as the story illustrates, carries cultural blindness to predictable tragedy.

So they [the missionary women] put her into the street. Already she had sold her loom. She had nothing more to sell except the single robe upon her back, and a few pair of useless *tabi*, or cleft stockings, which the missionary-women had obliged her to buy, because they thought that it was immodest for a young girl to be seen with naked feet.

"Perhaps," he adds, with a sardonic twist, "she existed only to furnish one example of facts that every foreign missionary ought to try to understand."[15]

Hearn did find occasional praise for that extraordinary missionary, the Philadelphian William Griffis: "Griffis is less inclined to beastliness than most of the wolfpack to which he belongs."[16] It would have been hard to dismiss this well-respected writer on Japan, who had arrived in 1869 to witness the beginnings of the Meiji era and whose interests often overlapped with Hearn's.[17] As Robert Rosenstone has described Griffis, he was a man confused by his experiences, almost for a time converted by the world he would convert,[18] and Griffis's accounts of his travels, deceiving and self-deceiving as they might have been, tell of wonder and awe. Hearn could sympathize with another man torn between two worlds, who had the courage to speak about the physical beauties and spiritual powers he witnessed.[19] Nevertheless, Griffis represented the hated clan, and Hearn's references to him are few.

In addition to missionaries, a diverse cross-section of foreigners came to live in Japan. Physicians such as William Willis or diplomats such as Algernon Mitford, residents in an earlier generation than Hearn, had experienced the stresses of British, French, and American efforts to impose diplomatic rights, among them the right to travel in distant parts. Mitford records one trip in which, for minor reasons of protocol, his Japanese hosts insisted on another route than the one he had planned, thereby avoiding ambush and murder at the hands of two hundred waiting samurai.[20] Willis details the conditions of prostitution, the incidence of venereal disease, and sundry unsavory aspects of life in the treaty ports. Despite his major accomplishments, among them the founding of Japan's first Western-style hospital, he suffered like Ernest Fenollosa and others who, as time went by, lost favor with the Japanese. Japan's adoption of German rather than British medical models left Willis with marginal influence in his later years.[21] He devoted himself to serving Japan and apparently enjoyed his life there (notwithstanding the fact that his huge bulk made him a Gulliver in Lilliput).

Hearn had little interest and no competence in practical matters, and, however much his earlier writings reached into science and technology, the Japanese books focus elsewhere. In this respect he followed Mitford, an editor of traditional Japanese stories and a writer of a long volume of memoirs, throughout a major portion of which Mitford nostalgically relived his life in the diplomatic service. Mitford's estate in England boasted a Japanese garden complete with rare specimens of bamboo and other plants from the country he had grown to love. Almost any literate visitor to Japan knew his collection of *Japanese Folk Tales* (1871), a pioneer introduction of such stories in the West, if not the full depiction of Japanese civilization that Mitford claimed it to be.[22] Mitford could extol Japanese art and folklore while asserting, with the Meiji government itself, Japan's need to catch up with material developments in the West. Again this was to prove an unresolved issue for Hearn, who chased after the folklore *and* urged a strong Japan while deploring changes imitative of the West.[23]

About the occasional travelers who, as Chamberlain says, churned out books after a few weeks' visit, Hearn had not much good to say. He seems to have read such literature as a matter of course, usually expressing his contempt for its shortsighted or patronizing views. One writer who should have interested him (she interested Chamberlain) and whose account of Japan involved his own sort of personal commitment gets passing, if complimentary, mention: "Miss Bird has well said that when one remains long in Japan, one finds one's standards of beauty changing."[24]

Isabella L. Bird's *Unbeaten Tracks in Japan,* published in 1880, which makes only passing reference to aesthetics, is an astonishing record of courage and independence. Traveling with a single, untrustworthy guide in 1878, Bird looked with a skeptical eye at everything from the tawdriness of Yokohama to the splendor of the temples at Nikko. She called her account a "narrative of travels" rather than "a Book on Japan" and "a study rather than a rapture." Bird describes varieties of topography, counts houses, assesses horses, records climatic conditions, and observes as dispassionately as she can the alien Japanese mores. Miffed, however, by the apparent indifference of Japanese peasants to what offends her sensibilities, she writes contemptuously about foul smells and bad health:

Would that these much-exposed skulls [of the villagers north of Nikko] were always smooth and clean! It is painful to see the prevalence of such repulsive maladies as *scabies,* scald-head, ringworm, sore eyes, and unwholesome-looking eruptions, and fully 30 per cent of the village people are badly seamed with smallpox.[25]

Bird worries about matters large and small that Hearn either doesn't see or doesn't object to. Insects may be a case in point. Bird leaves several attractive villages because she cannot stand the fleas or mosquitoes. With rare exceptions—he says at one point that "the insects in Kumamoto are great plagues"—Hearn's references to insects are positive, as his essays on "Fireflies," "Dragonflies," "Butterflies," "Ants," and "Mosquitoes" suggest.[26] His wife told of entering his study one evening and seeing several large insects draw blood from his bare back. Hearn had apparently not noticed them.[27] Certain types of discomfort and hence many topics common in Western visitors' reports scarcely entered the Japan he describes. He prefers to tell his readers about the sound of wooden sandals or the features of a little girl playing by a stream or the configurations on the shell of a crab. He insists on the ordinary—as he had through a long journalism career— with the ordinary transformed into something singular, a guidepost to the right observer. Even when writing about dust, the topic of one of his essays, dust becomes metaphorical, if not metaphysical, both the mundane grit stirred by the wheels of the jinrikisha and the stuff of dreams.

In the letters to her sister that became her book, Bird seeks to claim the *real* Japan, by which she does not mean, as Hearn would, the remnants of an idealized society. Or not entirely. Bird moved farther and farther north, across to Hokkaido, the distant and relatively unpeopled island that, for most Japanese, still hardly counted as Japan. Here she lived for several months among the Ainu, a Caucasian people thought by the Japanese to be uncivilized and banished to remote areas, their identity—and numbers— disappearing. She simulated anthropologists, who were elsewhere seeking out the most "primitive," the most exotic, the most authentic, in the hope of an anthropological charting of native life.[28] Despite its "ethnographic" penetration of an unknown Japan, Hearn would probably have disliked *Unbeaten Tracks* for its superior tone, its insufficiently generous point of view.[29] Yet he could, surprisingly, recommend Pierre Loti and Rudyard Kipling, who endorsed much that he deplored in Western parochialism.

2   For a stranger [in a foreign land] to cease to be a
         stranger he must stand ready . . . to pay with his
         person.
                                —Henry James, *Hawthorne*

A few years before Hearn's arrival in Japan, Pierre Loti (Julien Viaud), a young French naval officer, had fascinated audiences in the West with personal accounts of Japan. A writer who could not have been more different from Isabella Bird, Loti was Hearn's forerunner in popularizing Japanese topics, his *Madame Chrysanthème* testifying to the growing lure of Japan and *Japonisme* in Western lands.

Hearn not only shared the admiration for Loti, he also corresponded with Loti and drew on him for his own discovery of Japan. His translations of Loti's writings, including several that were later collected in *Japoneries d'Automne,* were actually the first English versions of Loti, and Hearn, who considered Loti "the most original of modern novelists," the writer whose "prose [was] more poetical than all English poetry," emulated Loti's manner.[30] The translations closely approximate Hearn's sensuous and exploratory style. Even granting that the language of the translations *is* Hearn's English, the parallels remain, suggesting an uncanny intimacy between Loti's impressions and Hearn's admiring renditions. "No writer," he says, "ever had such an effect on me."[31]

Madame Chrysanthème, Loti's best-known commentary on Japan, is no less arrogant for being a self-scrutinizing and self-deprecating book. Writing it first as a diary to record his shifting reactions, Loti later turned it into a loose and baggy narrative. *Madame Chrysanthème* tells the story of a brief interlude in Nagasaki, of "marriage" to a concubine, which is for Loti far more disturbing and dislocating than he can admit to himself.[32] He thinks (in company with Henry Adams) that the Japanese look and act like "monkeys": They are small, ugly, unknowable. Anticipating Joseph Conrad on Africa, he speaks of "hearts of darkness," the phrase suggesting a civilization permanently foreign to European sensibilities. Loti's sharp senses, Hearn recognized, allowed for "exquisite, weird, or wonderful" observations,[33] but his prejudices dominate *Madame Chrysanthème,* reducing it much of the time to petty self-indulgence: "Little, finical, affected,—all Japan is contained, both physically and morally, in these three words."[34]

In other moods (and when the rain stops) Loti grudgingly acknowledges his appreciation for selected bits of the country he had intended to love. With a clearly racist bias, he finds the children, and adult treatment of children, to be charming: "I am quite ready to admit," he says, "the attractiveness of the little Japanese children." Even when confessing to the pleasures of exotic difference, Loti undercuts his enthusiasms: "What a country of verdure and shade is Japan; what an unlooked-for Eden." Yet the landscape he depicts like a set for *The Mikado* (produced in 1885 at the time of Loti's arrival in Japan) frustrates him, tantalizing like some untouchable vision, the "untruthful aspect of too much prettiness." Recognizing more than the theatrical backdrop, he is troubled by a scarcely definable beauty, which is analogous to that of the young (eighteen-year-old?) woman with whom he lives. Because Madame Chrysanthème stays aloof, or maintains a sulky dignity, Loti admits to hating her. Japan the country finds its emblem in the woman he has exploited, and he sees both as shams: "A Japanese woman, deprived of her long dress and her huge sash with its pretentious bows, is nothing but a diminutive yellow being."[35]

For Loti, Japan is what so much of the Orient was to other travelers, both a release from another world and a promise of sexual pleasures, which intensified with the anonymity of the woman chosen for entertainment. Cohabiting with his diminutive "wife," he remains preoccupied by sex and entertainment, reminded continually of his own alien presence. Loti's insensitivity would be challenged by John Luther Long's story "Madame Butterfly" (1898), which became David Belasco's play; Giacomo Puccini saw and admired the play and turned it into his opera *Madama Butterfly* in 1904.[36] The three works offer tacit criticism of Loti's story and its exploitation of the Japanese woman because she seems (not speaking his language) unthinking or shallow. At the same time they subscribe to other Western illusions. Neither Long nor Puccini knew anything firsthand about the setting of their works, for neither had seen the Japan they chose to defend. In attempting to give moral and emotional stature to Japanese women, they perpetuated a stereotype of exotic otherness.

Apart from the Nagasaki episode, Loti's own response to Japanese women helped stimulate this sort of reverence. His later infatuation with the empress of Japan ("one of those few women who may be called, in the refined sense of the word, exquisite")[37] indicates that from a certain distance, or when social ranks were involved, he could admire Japanese women in a way that Hearn himself evidently did, idolizing beauty, haughtiness, or "grace," and sentimentalizing "fallen women."

But there is no question that Loti's infatuations emerge out of franker dialogues with himself about his wants and needs. Hearn, who often defends sensuality, may have appreciated both Loti's physical experiments in the country and his baffled sense of the land's beauty as well as his readiness to talk about matters that remained for Hearn more or less taboo. Although Hearn, too, accepted a marriage with a Japanese woman he barely knew, his written experiences seem at odds with those of Loti. When most under Loti's influence, on the other hand, he had thought about comparable writing: "I was in hopes that I might be able to contribute ['erotic papers']," he wrote to an editor in 1885, "on Oriental subjects to some leading magazine."[38] Except in the patterns of his metaphors, there is scarcely a hint of sexual topics in his published writings. Indeed, he says little about any of his physical needs, except occasionally about keeping cool or wanting to eat, and he remains circumspect about physical love. He speaks more easily and more abstractly about a woman's love or about woman-as-god,[39] and he singles out stories about faithful or exceptionally beautiful women. Private documents are another matter. A handwritten glossary from the time in Matsue spells out, presumably for a Japanese friend, a long list of colloquial American and English sexual terms in explicit detail.[40] Hearn may have suppressed such matters in public—or perhaps escaped them in the isolation of his study—but they remained no less important to his thinking.

In his notes for *Glimpses*, Hearn recounts a night in an inn when he was comforted and served by an attractive attendant (*nesan*), who allows his shy advances without reciprocating. He says of a journey in a jinrikisha: "And all the way I think I fondled that hand a little,—just as one presses occasionally the hand of a child with whom one is walking. She never returns the pressure, but remains absolutely, childishly, beautifully submissive."[41] Since in private letters Hearn confesses his own powerful eroticism,[42] his insistence on the woman's innocence and on his own honorable intentions suggests that he expected to incorporate the passage in *Glimpses*, having persuaded himself that her behavior defined his feelings. He may have come to realize that laconic comments about a sleepless night and loneliness raised questions inappropriate for his audience, which expected honesty but not frankness about physical desire. When incorporating surrounding passages from the notebook in *Glimpses*, he omitted this one.

Because in his public writings he will not allow himself what Loti most wants to explore, Hearn may be said to rewrite Loti—just as he replaced him as the mediator for Japan among Western readers. And here his choice of self-censorship works to his advantage. Whatever his fascination with race or empire,[43] he never consciously hints at exploitation, never looks down at either the men or the women he encounters. While admitting that Hearn was an important interpreter of Japan for a generation of Westerners, Donald Keene says that his attitude toward the Japanese was "patronizing."[44] Few writers were less patronizing, if *patronizing* means the insinuation of another's inferiority. Loti is patronizing, because Loti looks at Japanese people as if they were "toys" and "dolls" and "illusions."[45] Hearn looks with an intent to understand, with the assumption that it is he who must learn, that enigmas will remain enigmas, always beyond the reach of his own inadequate knowledge. This is not the whole story. Perhaps, after all, he was content with enigmas, taking satisfaction from the limits of his learning or needing a Japan that hearkened back to his childhood. In some contexts, moreover, he accepts the superiority of Western ideas, as his relentless praise for Herbert Spencer suggests. But there is here a kind of parallel adjustment, as if he is saying that Western ideas, the product of another sort of evolutionary development, are intellectually complete when united or at least compatible with Eastern spiritual values.

He knows, too, that his Western intellectuality has been altered radically by experiences in Japan. His remark to Basil Hall Chamberlain that he was "more and more impressed with the unspeculative character of the Japanese"[46] may be unwitting condescension, albeit common to many observers of Japan, but Hearn intends it as praise.[47] It was unspeculative thinking that allowed escape from the overly intellectual and historically bound categories of his Western heritage. More broadly, Japan as a whole may have allowed Hearn escape from what he thought lesser or lower selves (in the vocabulary of the time), as if he were responding to a higher standard of behavior as well as ideas.

In any case, when he struggles to understand Japanese life, Hearn does not assume, as Loti does, that Japan is at fault. This is true whether he speaks of religion, people, literature, the visual arts, or politics. If Hearn patronizes anybody, it is fellow visitors to Japan, especially those trading in Japanese artifacts or in facile interpretations or in jingoistic arrogance. His conviction remains that only someone observant and ready to spend time with the Japanese can possibly make sense of their customs or intuit their civilization. Even with sympathy, the task is likely to fail. "Who," he says, "can do justice to Japan without sympathy; and how many writers on Japan have a grain of it? . . . What a horribly difficult thing it is to write about Japan. The effort in itself dries me up."[48]

Given the differences between them, it is not surprising that Hearn came to a less ecstatic estimate of Loti (who later snubbed his letters) and of Loti's works, which he found finally uninteresting. He wrote in 1893: "To me Loti seems for a space to have looked into Nature's whole burning fulgurant soul. . . . Then the color and the light faded, and only the worn-out blasé nerves remained."[49] Yet some of Loti's talents must have remained attractive, among them his absorption in his own memories, which, like Hearn's, inform his entire perspective:

I refer too often, I fancy, to my childhood; I am foolishly fond of it. But it seems to me that then only did I truly experience sensations or impressions; the smallest trifles I then saw or heard were full of deep and hidden meaning, recalling past images out of oblivion, and reawakening memories of prior existences; or else they were presentiments of existences to come, future incarnations in the land of dreams. . . . Well, I have grown up, and have found nothing that answered to all my indefinable expectations. . . . All has narrowed and darkened around me.[50]

Loti's emphasis on the power of childhood memories and of memories beyond the personal once again sounds like the language of Hearn himself. Japan, which both at times describe as Edenic, also disappoints, and for Loti, as for Hearn, the escape into Japan becomes another reminder of life's disillusionment, its failure to satisfy. Perhaps more than Hearn, Loti distinguishes between the pattern itself and his experience in Japan. Hearn usually defines his state of mind as a function of his satisfaction or dissatisfaction with his adopted country. "What worries me," he writes (with a characteristic leap of logic) "is the absence of feeling,—the want of something to stir one profoundly when his knowledge of the country is sufficient to prevent illusion. And it won't come. I must content myself with the queer, the curious, . . .—or attempt a work on Buddhism."[51]

The exclusion of certain feelings, the tentative autobiographical approach to experience, and the reluctance to explore obvious areas of struggle and discomfort characterize Hearn's books. Much is omitted, even in the exploration of Hearn's personal Japan. The first chapter of his 1896 book *Kokoro: Hints and Echoes of Japanese Inner Life*

(*Kokoro* means "of the heart") is representative. From a perspective he used consistently in his journalistic pieces in Cincinnati and New Orleans, Hearn tells of the return of a murderer to the city where, several years before, he had killed a young father. When the murderer appears in the railroad station, he must face not just a large crowd but also the victim's widow and her son. Hearn himself speaks as a witness. He describes in detail how the murderer responds to the situation, broken down by shame and remorse when confronting the child: "I saw the prisoner's features distort; I saw him suddenly dash himself down upon his knees despite his fetters, and beat his face into the dust, crying out the while in a passion of hoarse remorse that made one's heart shake."[52]

Hearn's vivid account encompasses both the crowd and the individuals in it whose feelings he reads from gestures, dialogue, and facial expressions. Since Hearn performs as observer and narrator, the story comes across as obliquely personal, even passionate, though it reveals far less about Lafcadio Hearn than it illustrates—with all the drama and public emotion Hearn can realize—sympathetic trespass into the hearts of others. By limiting feelings to the generic and subordinate, as "one's heart" implies, Hearn mutes the range of emotions presumably felt by the man who writes.

3 And west you'll turn and south again, beyond the sea-fog's rim,
   And tell the Yoshiwara[53] *girls to burn a stick for him*. . . .
  There is more art in that one line [of Kipling] than in all "Madame Chrysanthème."
   —Hearn to Basil Hall Chamberlain, 31 October 1893

Just as Hearn's reticence sets him apart from Loti, his personal engagement sets him apart from Rudyard Kipling, who took Loti's place in his pantheon of great authors. In the year before Hearn's arrival, Kipling, passing through Japan on his way from India, had published a series of letters that Hearn considered to be unequaled. Indeed, Kipling emerged as the contemporary author who moved him most and confronted him with his own deficiencies: "Goodness! how small it makes me feel to read that man." And he did read Kipling: "I have read most of his books four or five times over; and some particular stories much oftener. I like nearly everything."[54] Despite such protestations, his acceptance came hard, no doubt for the reason that Kipling's sensibility differed so markedly from his own. "I feel I still underrate Kipling," he wrote to Mason in 1892. "He grows bigger every day to me—looms up colossally—reaches out like a stupendous shadow, over half a planet at once. But oh! the hardness of the tone—the silent cynicism of facts—the self-repression—the matter-of-course way of seeing things!"[55]

A young journalist at the time of his visit in 1889, Kipling was already used to asking questions and pushing beyond the obvious. In contrast to Hearn, who at first imitated Western tourists by running after shrines and temples, he confessed to a limited taste for such things and wanted to know more about the practical side of the country—for instance, its entry into the industrialized world. He asked about the new constitution of Japan (instituted in 1889, a few weeks before his visit), the development of the railways, and the terms of the agreements that opened treaty ports to the West. Practical questions did not curb his curiosity about Japanese prints, buildings, theater, and eating habits. Kipling also relished Japanese food, unlike most of his compatriots, who, when they left the "civilization" of the treaty ports, were careful to pack their Leibig's Extract of Beef and other satisfactorily reliable foods—along with the solace of Keating's Flea Powder.[56]

Kipling, who made only two brief visits to Japan, arrived with a less generous attitude than Hearn's. Here, for instance, he writes about a jinrikisha ride:

The walk to the Consulate exhausted the European portion of Kobe, and the Professor [S. A. Hill, a friend from India] and I went away to the Japanese town in 'rickshaws. The one man in the shafts was a curiosity. He began running on level ground as swiftly as though he was a whole team of *paharis* [Indian term for "hillman"]. This vexed me and I gave him a half-mile on the flat, down the street. He stopped full of running. Then I ran him back again and finished with an ascent. He ran up that and said there was a curio-shop at five minutes' distance. He was clad in a blue jerkin, knee breeches and blue gaiters, and his number was painted on his back. Whence he drew his powers of endurance I cannot tell, but he ran eternally for ten cents an hour while I studied Japan.[57]

In a comparable passage from *Glimpses of Unfamiliar Japan*, Hearn watches his driver more fully than Kipling does, and he writes with keener sympathy, naming the man and seeing him *as* a man:

My kurumaya [rickshaw driver] calls himself "Cha." He has a white hat which looks like the top of an enormous mushroom; a short blue wide-sleeved jacket; blue drawers, close-fitting as "tights," and reaching to his ankles; and light straw sandals bound upon his bare feet with cords of palmetto-fibre. Doubtless he typifies all the patience, endurance, and insidious coaxing powers of his class. He has already manifested his power to make me give him more than the law allows; and I have been warned against him in vain. For the first sensation of having a human being for a horse, trotting between shafts, unwearyingly bobbing up and down before you for hours, is alone enough to evoke in you a feeling of compassion. And when this human being . . . with all his hopes, memories, sentiments, and comprehensions, happens to have the gentlest smile, . . . this compassion becomes sympathy.[58]

Whereas Kipling treats the driver as if he were a horse, Hearn consciously probes the implications of the metaphor: what it means for a human being to serve in the capacity of a horse. The man's degradation may not persuade him to walk; it does sensitize him to matters of class and privilege, forcing him beyond specific details to a richer appreciation of the society as a whole. This makes for a more complete, more fully human, observation. (It is worth adding that Hearn draws from his early notes in Japan, from a time, that is, when he was as unfamiliar with the country as Kipling had been during his brief visit.) As Chamberlain noted, Kipling can be intensely "graphic," a shrewd and careful observer;[59] Hearn himself said much the same thing. Still Kipling's attitudes are those of a superior, his ironic look at the sinewy and robotic driver a negative equivalent of Hearn's empathic hyperbole.

Kipling sometimes directed irony at himself, more often at the country or its natives, whom he saw from a detached, perhaps even an Indian-imperial perspective.[60] Alert as he was to so many of the prejudices of his countrymen, Kipling commended the mission of foreign traders. He recognized in the Westerners he met in Japan the stalwart breed he had admired in Bombay and Singapore, in the clubs reserved for European businesspeople that lay scattered around port cities of the Far East. It fell to Western traders to represent the best interests of the home country, to serve as unpopular but necessary instruments of Western progress. To be sure, they had privileges, he told a group of them on his second visit in 1892, and they deserved all they got.

I meet here, if not the very same men, at least the very same type of men as those among whom I have been bred and trained, . . . men afar and apart from the surroundings and supports of their own countries, but playing no small part in their countries' greatness; those who are the builders of trade, the makers of ways, and the teachers of all good influences; each upholding and advancing the honour and the dignity of his country.[61]

Despite Hearn's guarded praise for the Anglo-American communities when loneliness in Kumamoto made him long for the treaty ports or when he wrote editorials for the Kobe *Chronicle*, he would never have considered fellow Westerners to be "the teachers of all good influences." Just the contrary. With the exception of his brief visits with Mitchell McDonald in Yokohama, he chose either Japanese company or, more commonly, no company at all. Westerners embodied a large part of what he disliked about the new and future Japan.

4   In America and Europe he cannot be looked upon as a
     mere searcher after exotics. His mind was constantly
     filled with parallels and comparisons between eastern
     and western art.
                              —Ezra Pound on Ernest Fenollosa

Perhaps the visitors to Japan whom Hearn most closely approximates are Ernest Fenollosa, who (with Edward S. Morse) helped Japan rediscover its artistic heritage after the excessive Westernization of the early Meiji years, and Percival Lowell, another Harvard graduate who found his richest education in the East. Coming to Japan with other purposes and with limited sympathy—as Van Wyck Brooks pointed out long ago—Morse and Fenollosa grew to love the country and to admire its non-Western qualities.[62] They became collectors as well as students, developing plans for artistic holdings and future museums. Hearn also collected Japanese artifacts, especially pipes (*kiseru*) and cheap prints, although his main love in the arts centered on the ephemeral: small bits of folk art made quickly and unpretentiously, such things as children's handmade toys, kites, and folded paper.

Hearn's assessment of Japan rested on a haunting awareness of fragility. Perhaps with his own pattern of change in mind, he argued that Japanese homes were designed not to last: They reflected the imminence of earthquakes, violent weather, and other natural catastrophes endemic to the islands.[63] Much as he admired the "funny little things" of Japan, Hearn was not a compulsive or a trained connoisseur of pottery and other traditional Japanese arts. For Morse and Fenollosa, who were, Japan remained a consuming part of their lives while at the same time a step toward later careers. Both public men gladly advised and accepted power, and they sought out others similarly inclined, thereby making their own alternative community to the Western groups that, like Hearn, they tended to avoid.

In converting to Buddhism, Fenollosa committed himself to Japan even more deeply than did Hearn, who admired Buddhism while regretting that he could only accept it intellectually. Visiting Japan with the painter John La Farge—and with immovable skepticism about Japan—Henry Adams poked fun at Fenollosa's religious fervor in letters home: "He has joined a Buddhist sect," said Adams. "I was myself a Buddhist when I left America, but he has converted me to Calvinism with leanings towards the Methodists."[64] Convert and enthusiast that he was, Fenollosa indulged in arbitrary excellences, as if to establish his own clear tastes in the massive fields of Asian arts. Refusing at first to acknowledge the merits of any Japanese art produced in the Tokugawa era (1600–1868), he amused Adams by insisting—principles aside—on a tour of Nikko, famous for the elaborate Tokugawa artwork of its temples and tombs.

Fenollosa, who had lived in Japan for about a decade when he and Hearn met in the spring of 1890, gained enormous popularity with the Japanese, whether high government officials or colleagues at Tokyo Imperial University. At the 1940 celebration of Hearn in Japan, one former university colleague wrote that "an American, Mr. Ernest Fenollosa, stands out in my memory. . . . At that time I failed to appreciate Mr. Koizumi's work."[65] Fenollosa evidently appreciated Hearn. The two men recognized in each other kindred spirits, and Hearn, with his usual spontaneous enthusiasm, admired Fenollosa, writing to him about Japan's "witchcraft," its almost alchemic ability "to transform cheapness itself into luxury incomparable."[66] Since Fenollosa left Japan soon after, they were not to meet again for several years. When they did meet on Fenollosa's return from Boston, their positions were oddly reversed. Now Hearn was the professor, Fenollosa more or less the outsider. Earlier Japanese friendliness toward Fenollosa had diminished, perhaps as a part of the late-century shift away from Western enthusiasms, perhaps as a result of subtle distancing within Fenollosa himself. In any case, this man, who had been honored by the emperor and praised as the savior of Japanese art, found himself neither able to find a reasonable job nor much sought after for his expertise. He might have said with Hearn (but did not): "I have been treated very cruelly by the Japanese."[67] Because Hearn by 1898 had become an almost total recluse, the two may have had even more in common than at the time of their earlier meeting. Fenollosa had learned to accept Hearn's now common appreciation of popular Japanese arts—especially ukiyo-e, the subject of one of his books—branching out from his exclusive love of ancient and more aristocratic modes.[68]

Uncharacteristically, and as a sign of his affection, Hearn visited Fenollosa's lodgings. Mrs. Fenollosa recorded his arrival and its effect on the family:

[Hearn] got here about 2:30. Anne [Dyer, a friend and collaborator of Mary Fenollosa] and I of course kept out of the way. We heard E. greet him cordially. . . . About an hour later E. came bounding upstairs, his face radiant and cried, "Oh, he is splendid. I love him as I do Okakura. He will see you. He *wants* to see you. It is a delight to see such a man!" Of course I hurried down. I had put on my Japanese kimono and tea gown thinking it would be a subtle compliment. As this was my first sight of him, I will try to de-scribe the effect. A small man of grey tone with delicate, slightly distorted features and with his entire personality warped, twisted a little to the right, the result, I suppose, of his semi-blindness and poor eyesight. He was thinner and smaller than I had thought, and his hair is very grey. The white, blind left eyeball is a terrible defect and one feels always his consciousness of this. . . . But his beautiful voice—sweet, vibrating—never loud nor piercing—has an irresistible charm—and as one knows him better and begins to feel that the shy spirit is creeping more and more from its fragile shell—one ceases to care for anything material. As Anne said, he carries his own environment with him.[69]

Fenollosa may not have been aware that Hearn seldom visited anyone or that, except for necessary trips to the university, he insisted on staying at home. So his visit itself paid tribute to a fellow advocate for the old Japan, to another displaced outsider in less gracious years of the late century. After the war with China and the swing back to a more independent political position, Japan had ended its call for people like Fenollosa and Hearn, as it had for Dr. Willis. They were now tolerated instead of welcomed.

Mary Fenollosa's account gives a good sense of the frail, self-conscious Hearn, whose enthusiasms proved infectious and who, to someone like Fenollosa, served to embody his own sympathetic principles. (Mary Fenollosa nevertheless admits that, for all their appreciation of Herbert Spencer, she and her husband maintained a discreet silence when Hearn made the connection—to them entirely specious—between Spencer and Buddhism.)

The observation that Lafcadio Hearn carried his environment with him is both astute and overstated. It had been Hearn's own opinion, as he had written many years before to his friend George Gould: "I inherit certain susceptibilities, weaknesses, sensitivenesses, which render it impossible to adapt myself to the ordinary *milieu;* I have to make one of my own, wherever I go, and never mingle with that already made."[70] Hearn's ambition, and his practice in Cincinnati or New Orleans, had been to "mingle" professionally and socially with "ordinary" people but also to keep to himself, to create his own separate and interior world. Something of an exception for him, Japan provided a temporary illusion of adaptation in an *extra*ordinary milieu.

5   Your lines about Lowell almost put him into my room, and I think I can hear him talk. Now for some presumption. He is so much larger a man than I, that I would feel it presumption to differ with him on any point if I did not remember that in the psychological world a man may grow too tall to see anything near him clearly.
         —Hearn to Basil Hall Chamberlain, 14 January 1893

If it is true that Hearn carried his environment with him, we can think of him defining his idea of Japan—and his own role in Japan—as a function of his reading. He spoke of the devastating effect of Kipling's writing and the frustration because Loti had preempted his own impressions of Kyoto or forced his perceptions. Hearn's remarks to Chamberlain about books he had read (and he read widely, however modest he was about his accomplishments) mainly attested to the emotional effect a particular author had upon him. Gautier and Poe were two profound influences in company with Kipling and Loti. Another was Percival Lowell, author of *The Soul of the Far East* (1888).

Along with the translations he made from Loti's *Japoneries d'Automne*, Lowell's book may have provided the most compelling arguments for Hearn's final voyage.[71] Well before the opportunity arose of a trip to Japan, Hearn had written to George Gould that Lowell's book was "divine poetry [touching] only that which no scientific knowledge can explain—that which must remain mysterious"[72]—a willful reading, given Lowell's scientific interests and his habit of debunking the mysteries. Hearn's experiences in Japan confirmed his opinion of Lowell, who remained for him a guide to the spiritual and intangible qualities he sought in Japanese life. To his friend Mason he wrote in July 1892: "The force of Lowell's 'Soul of the Far East' is daily growing on me. . . . There are times I feel so hopeless about everything in Japan that I would like to leave it if I had no one else to care for."[73]

The discontinuity between Hearn's praise for Lowell and his admission of hopelessness typifies his letters. In the first place, while he put aside his skepticism and believed at one point that he had found his soul in Japan, his life never seemed to him to have the clarity and purpose he saw in Lowell, who always spoke with authority and had a good command of Japanese.[74] His hold on Japan proved at once more tenuous, or unsure, and more tenacious, as if he had committed himself to the country, regardless of what he had lost. Part of the reason for his commitment to Japanese life was his conviction that, wherever the new Japan might be going, the old Japan had found both beauty and morality, achieving a higher civilization than was imaginable in the individualistic and competitive West. How Eastern civilization should evolve, except in parody of the West, Hearn hardly touches on, largely because—while admiring Japan for its ability to change—he prefers to believe in enduring values. Still, as he said to Chamberlain, beliefs are lent to us for a brief time; illusions are as fleeting as they are necessary.

Hearn differed from writers like Chamberlain, who remained unswervingly, if less passionately, attached to Japan; and from writers like Lowell, who knew when to leave.[75] However much Lowell may have escaped from his homeland or assumed for a time a certain Eastern superiority, he professed time and again that Western individualism, a demonstrated effect of evolution, situated the West on a higher plane of development. Such a premise led him to an arbitrary distinction between taste and creativity, the one being key to the arts of the East, the other a distinguishing and superior quality limited to the West. Lowell's unoriginal conclusion suggests little, as one shrewd commentator puts it, except "that in his own case keen passing observation should be distinguished from knowledge in depth of a culture and its history."[76]

Hearn at times associates imagination with individuality, with "genius," and he may unwittingly think that—because it could breed philosophers like Herbert Spencer—his own native culture(s) had the edge over that of Japan. He tried to show, however, that the East had long anticipated Western thought, possibly excelling it. As for Eastern creativity, he was convinced of its superiority in several respects. He admired folk arts, which he thought were lost in the West. He took delight in Japanese tales—poems, ghost stories, religious lore—as any of his books from Japan affirm. There may be no question that to Hearn Western writers like Shakespeare inhabited an altogether superior realm of creativity (so much so that his lectures to

Tokyo University undergraduates allowed only a complementary role for Eastern literatures), yet it is also true that
Hearn understood Shakespeare as an incorporative genius,
a composite "intellectual memory," whose talents sub-
sumed those of contemporaries and of ancestors. In other
words, Hearn appreciated Shakespeare in the collective
ways he and others tended to reserve for Eastern artistic
traditions.

As Chamberlain observed, Hearn's thinking remained
open, whereas Lowell's did not: "Say not a word against
'modernity' in [Lowell's] presence, or you will catch it. . . .
His plan is to argue down deductively from some general
notion, such as the supreme virtue of 'modernity,' the 'im-
personality of Orientals,' etc., . . . and then bend the facts
to suit the preconceived idea."[77] More loyal to writers than
to people, Hearn could fault Lowell only for an occasional
lack of sympathy—or Olympian detachment.

In *Occult Japan*, a book that in some ways resembles
Hearn's *Japan: An Attempt at Interpretation* (1904),
Lowell begins, as Hearn often does, with a personal narrative (a climb up a holy mountain). Here the physical journey represents a search for authentic experience and for
guidance into larger questions of Japanese faith, above all
the mysteries of Buddhism and Shintoism:

We had reached, after various vicissitudes, as prosaically as possible in unprosaic Japan, a height of about nine thousand feet [on
Otake, "the honorable peak"], when we suddenly came upon a
manifestation as surprising as it was unsuspected. Regardless of
us, the veil was thrown aside, and we gazed into the beyond. We
stood face to face with the gods.[78]

Both Hearn and Lowell dwell on small and indicative
detail, facial expressions, temperature, fragments of legend
or history. Lowell's assessment, while it gives a lived sense
of extraordinary encounters, usually turns incredulous.
After detailing the progress of several Shinto miracles,
Lowell carefully explains that salt takes heat from live
coals or that Japanese feet are exactly suited to withstand
the sharp edges of swords or that the theater of public

miracles plays to an audience more than ready to accept the spiritual power of what it sees. Not only is Lowell skeptical, his skepticism takes the form of irony, the laughter of which he directs at those who are gullible and at the skilled practitioners who, if they do not dupe, certainly sway their audiences like so many skilled entertainers. Presumably their task is made all the easier because "impersonal" people, the Japanese, seem "never to have grown up."[79]

The record of his personal journey and his encounter with Shinto rites notwithstanding, Lowell emerges within a few pages as an authority, making judgments beyond what he can empirically attest to, pronouncing on the truth or value for an audience he assumes to be of his own kind. His humor has an occasional edge, as if to say that *we*, as Westerners, can agree about the failings of Japanese superstition, regardless of how charming we find the customs or the people. "Survival of the unfittest" is the rule in a land where people "copy" rather than originate and where a Western notion of "development [has] ceased."[80]

For Hearn, on the contrary, Western superiority is a myth to be challenged, Japanese beauty and grace qualities to be demonstrated. His approach speaks to an altogether different purpose—with a different audience in mind. It is not that Hearn writes for the Japanese, rather that he writes with their judgment in mind.[81] He would want his friends Sentarō Nishida or Nobushige Amenomori to approve his description, to see it as another important phase in what may well be—indeed, proves to be—a futile attempt to penetrate the interior qualities of Japanese life. If Lowell with his agile mind knows a great deal, Lowell seems closed to what Hearn never doubts: the fundamental seriousness of the matters he studies. In exchange, of course, he can laugh and entertain, as Hearn no longer tried to do. "To speak backwards, write backwards, read backwards," Lowell writes, "is but the *a. b. c.* of their contrariety."[82] Hearn gives the impression that he has pushed himself as far as possible toward a privileged or exclusive otherness, the value of which he never publicly questions:

> As for myself, whenever I am alone in the presence of a Shinto shrine, I have the sensation of being haunted; and I cannot help thinking about the possible apperceptions of the haunter. And this tempts me to fancy how I should feel if I myself were a god,— dwelling in some old Izumo shrine on the summit of a hill, guarded by stone lions and shadowed by a holy grove. . . .
>
> As air to the bird, as water to the fish, so would all substance be permeable to the essence of me. I would pass at will through the walls of my dwelling to swim in the long gold bath of a sunbeam, to thrill in the heart of a flower, to ride on the neck of a drag-onfly.[83]

What he offers as commentary on the world he sees may be hyperbolic or ingenuous, as if written by someone who neither comprehends the mystery nor presumes to explain it for his audience. At the same time, the man who imagines himself as god or fish or bird enters fully into a vital world and passes at will through walls of convention. Neither Fenollosa nor Kipling nor Loti nor any other writers whom Hearn (at times abjectly) admired came close to this power.

[3]
The Japanbook

1   It is a mistake to think of Hearn as "a writer on
     Japan." Japan gave him nothing. . . . He himself, not
     Japan, is the interesting subject.
     —Albert Mordell, *An American Miscellany*

If Hearn's Japanese writings amount to one book, that book
has great diversity. Between *Glimpses of Unfamiliar Japan*, the product of Hearn's life in Matsue, and *Japan: An
Attempt at Interpretation* much had happened to Lafcadio
Hearn. The intoxicated singer of the first book had faced
and admitted to disillusion, and what had been half-
promised in private letters finally materialized: a study of
Japanese religions that was less a tribute to Hearn's
achieved spirituality than a sign of reduced ambition, an
acceptance of at least partial failure. Even the man's habits
had changed dramatically: He who had been whisked, as if
in fairyland, from temple to temple now stayed home in
the privacy of his study, thinking about those temples instead of visiting them, living increasingly in an imaginative space of his own making.[1] In all likelihood the focus
on religion signified Hearn's loss of those bursts of pleasure
coming from initiation into the secrets of Japan, just as it
was an admission of his inability to believe in the Buddhist
or Shinto faiths about which he was writing. Hearn's
posthumously published study is, if not dispirited,
markedly less enthusiastic than his earlier writings. It is
also the closest he came to what most readers would see as
an academic book.
     Some critics have felt that Hearn wrote his best work
relatively early in his Japanese years and that the later

Hearn preferred wearing Japanese dress. Notice the characteristic turn from the camera to hide his blind eye. *Courtesy of the Lafcadio Hearn Memorial Museum, Matsue, Japan; and of Mr. Toki Koizumi and Mr. Bon Koizumi.*

books merely continue the established pattern.[2] Such judgments are as hard to rebut as they are to prove. Kenneth Rexroth thinks Hearn's writings about Buddhism are unsurpassed in both range and clarity, and some of the most probing of these works came late in his career.[3] My sense is that, while Hearn may have become repetitive or perhaps less innovative as time went by, his later writings are as perceptive as the earlier works, and they may gain from the bleaker view of Japan—and of life itself—that they express. Probably, as Hearn himself felt, they are more complex than the enchanted accounts of Matsue and Lake Shinji and the beautiful temples of Izumo. The man who had long before described himself as devoted to the odd and exotic, the weird and the shocking, came increasingly to a deeper sense of Japan's richness, although with shifting enthusiasms. These writings are, nonetheless, of a piece. Stylistically as well as in substance, his dozen books on Japan make up one integral work, one long exploration of the writer himself and of the country he discovered.

Hearn's books consist of complementary parts: "reshaped tales from the Japanese"—stories, anecdotes, historical episodes—which dominate some books (such as *Kwaidan*), and the trials, experiments, or "little essays," as Hearn calls them, "offered merely as intimations of a truth," which make up nearly all of the others (such as *Exotics and Retrospectives* [1898]).[4] The two may alternate as parts of the same piece, the commentary introduced parenthetically in the stories, for example, or the stories illustrating Hearn's essayistic discussions. In *Glimpses of Unfamiliar Japan* the blending of the two goes further, with Hearn telling his own stories of trial and discovery, as if they themselves had become legends of a Westerner in Japan.

Albert Camus wrote in his *Notebooks* that a novel is only philosophy put into images: "People think only in images. If you want to be a philosopher, write novels."[5] Hearn wanted to write novels, and he associated novels with philosophy, or at least said that he only liked novels that were philosophical. But he thought intensely and chronically in images, and he apparently attempted no extended fictional work in Japan. With the possible exception of *Japan*, all his books are collections, and none professes to sustained argument, just as none allows a full disclosure of Lafcadio Hearn the man, though Hearn alludes throughout to his own complicated self, or selves. A great number of his essays speak about issues of personality, which he accepts as the generative force behind his writing and as a paradox that almost dismantles writing. He subscribes, that is, to nineteenth-century European assumptions about genius and imagination making art possible while acknowledging Eastern beliefs in the folly of all such illusions. This is perhaps another reason his works consist so entirely of fragments, some of them addenda to previous paragraphs, tails added to the tiny body of associative argument.

Revery is the word Hearn finds to describe the process of his daydream contemplations, the shifting states of mind which his writings both explore and record. For the Urashima story a sunny afternoon recalls an earlier time, which evokes a dream, then a vignette, and brings Hearn round to his often luminous but abstracted observation about Japan, collective memory, or the shape of his life. Some of the reveries are not essays, as such. Like the Urashima story, they may dwell on folklore and legend. Often speaking of things ghostly, they can also recount tales of contemporary Japan or enter philosophical explorations of culture and history.

What was and was not left out of these works? Their titles announce parts and pieces: "glimpses," "miscellanies," "attempts," "gleanings." There are repeated "shadowings," to use his own title for a collection, and shadowings imply at once limited sight on the one hand and stylistic or mnemonic shadings on the other.

A typical example of Hearn's books is *Kotto: Being Japanese Curios, with Sundry Cobwebs* (1902), the title itself a form of apology or at least a sign of the piecemeal nature of

the work or the self-protective advertisement of the author, who announces modest achievement. On the other
hand, the advertisement accurately tells what to expect in
the way of contents. Hearn includes the story of a young
woman who dares to steal the money box of a local god and
loses her child in the effort; an unfinished story, "In a Cup
of Tea," about a man who inadvertently swallows a ghost
and suffers more than indigestion; the story of a deluded
priest who confuses a vision of a bodhisattva with that of a
badger and is disabused of his folly by a worldly-wise hunter; another story of a merchant whose employee almost
dies because of the hatred of the merchant's wife; an account of a ghost who returns to save his honor and his
family's wealth; a story of another ghost who has extracted
a promise of fidelity from her husband and reappears night-
ly to destroy his new love; a story of a young girl who
returns from death as a fly to secure appropriate last rites;
and several other narratives from folklore and collections
of legends. In addition to narratives, Hearn offers "A Woman's Diary," a sympathetic transcription of a contemporary housewife's struggle with urban poverty; an essay on
crabs and their appearances; a semiscientific essay on fireflies; an essay on dewdrops, which becomes speculation on
life and personality; an essay on goblins (*gaki*); and a "Revery," about mother-love made infinite as the Oriental alternative to grim, patriarchal Western notions of God. There
are other pieces, some of them borrowed stories, some accounts of his own dreams and experiences. Whatever their
specific topic, all in a sense introduce a "shadow" self
straining for definition in a world half-hidden and half-
understood.

This and the chapter to follow explore the two complementary approaches in Hearn's Japanese writings, the
projections of his shadow self. I shall come back to some of
the stories; here my focus is on three impressionistic
pieces from *Exotics and Retrospectives* (1898), *Out of the
East* (1897), and *In Ghostly Japan* (1899).

"Fuji-no-Yama," from *Exotics*, records Hearn's 1897

climb of Mount Fuji, undertaken about halfway through his Japanese years. The essay is typical of Hearn's essays and also exceptional, because more personal, or more obviously revealing of the man's experience in Japan. Ordinary as Hearn insists his experience to be, and recognizing himself as merely another pilgrim on a common journey, he looks with idiosyncratic sharpness. More than a journey, the ascent of Fuji compels grudging self-exploration, however masked or unwanted.

The Fuji essay, as Hearn announces, draws from contemporary notes, which he has later "amended and expanded" to give them form and sequence without losing the vitality of an immediate response.[6] While typical of many writers, the process in his case tells much about the man and his work. To read Hearn's original notebooks—often small, cheap writing pads—can mean suffering through scribbled, occasionally illegible penciled comments accompanied by lists of Japanese words that are at once evidence of Hearn's continued efforts to learn the language and a sign of his lifelong love of naming. When Hearn's manuscripts are carefully written, the handwriting is clear and handsome, similar to the style of his personal letters. The notebooks are full of hurried entries that were later transcribed into texts for magazines and book publishers; he simply canceled the notes used for publication with a line down the center of the page.

In an early study of Hearn, Nina H. Kennard described at some length the writer's habits of revision, insisting that he worked and reworked, honing materials until finally satisfied.[7] This is true in a limited sense. He prided himself on expert polishing, and whenever possible he took great care with proofs, which he considered to be the most important stage of the revising process. Not to be able to read proof always irritated him, as if the essence of the project had been withheld.[8] But in spite of his passion about style and format, his writings were often transcriptions of early drafts rather than the products of elaborate rewriting, and—as with the beginning of *Glimpses*—Hearn calls attention to their scattered origins. The account of the Fuji experience, in this way typical, offers both the immediacy of the experience and its shock of discovery. As with *Two Years in the French West Indies* and *Glimpses* (for which he constructed belated notes and impressions), the essay develops along unexpected tangents, even at right angles.

Hearn introduces the ascent of Fuji as another "well-trodden," almost hackneyed topic because such a celebrated part of Japanese religious life. Villagers, he says, converge from across Japan to climb the mountain sacred to Buddhists and Shintoists alike:

> If this act of faith cannot be performed by everybody in person, it can at least be performed by proxy. Any hamlet, however remote, can occasionally send one representative to pray before the holy shrine of the divinity of Fuji, and to salute the rising sun from that sublime eminence.

The perspective announces Hearn as the self-appointed representative from even more remote regions, recounting his experience for all of us. So much has already been written about the mountain, he says, that "there is really very little left for me to tell about Fuji except my own experience of climbing it,"[9] and this is precisely what he had said about Japan itself as a topic before leaving America. Beginning with the assertion of his own limitations and the mundane nature of what he tells, he manages to make his personal encounter a key to general experience. For Hearn rarely does anything without establishing that other feet have trod before him, that he speaks for voices lost, and that he touches a universal common ground, religious, aesthetic, or emotional. His account, in other words, is both assertively personal and implicitly collective. This is why a reader like Stefan Zweig could think of Hearn as the appropriate Western speaker for things Japanese: No one else felt that his or her own experiences so nearly enacted a shared endeavor.

The long climb becomes for Hearn a way of coming to terms with an intrinsically Japanese event—though with a difference. Or, rather, with many differences, one of which is his isolating and inescapable role as outsider. Awaiting his guides in Gotemba, the nondescript village to the east of the mountain, he is unable to sleep. Here as in other essays he tells of noisy guests in the inn, of alien voices breaking the night's silence, often, as with the "fornicators" he describes elsewhere, in celebration of shared pleasures. When before sunrise the *goriki* (guides) arrive to instruct him, they force him to change clothes, to prepare fully—and hence emotionally—for a mountain that can seem like January in July, insisting on warm clothing and on Hearn's recognition that no ordinary walk lies ahead. The guides come to serve, to cater to someone who at this point plays an awkwardly passive role. They attend to his food, his clothing, his transportation to the mountain. For the first few miles, Hearn rides in a *kuruma* pulled by native servants, just as he had on his first day in Japan. Here, too, figuratively speaking, his approach to holy places is on the backs of the Japanese.

The essay on Fuji serves as an allegory of Hearn's spiritual and physical transition to being Japanese (he had by this time accepted Japanese citizenship). Imperially conveyed to the base of the mountain, he learns like a beginner to walk, and when forced to think about his life and his encounter with the alien culture his emotional struggle parallels the physical. The guides support him a long way up the mountain, beyond the area where the *kuruma* can travel or where he can be carried on horseback, prodding and tugging him up the long slopes. Despite his physical weakness, Hearn becomes increasingly independent of the *goriki,* if not forgetting his incapacitating fatigue, at least turning from it more and more to speculate about the mountain he climbs, about those who have climbed before and what it all might mean. Although a sustained narrative, less whimsical or interrupted than some of Hearn's essays, "Fuji-no-Yama" resembles the others in its uncertainty, its reluctance to define meaning or to sum up. Like so many other anecdotes, it points in a number of directions and ends with an indefinite understanding of the topics raised. There are at least two voices in this essay: what might be thought of as Western and Japanese voices, Hearn's agonistic expressions of unresolved conflict. He is more assertive and more paradoxical in his Western voice, more accepting and patient in his Eastern one, neither of which entirely prevails.

2   There is really an art in Gautier that lifts every word
         into the world of thinking, and that makes me almost
         ready to believe in a new Gnosticism—that words are
         Beings which reveal their souls only to the elect.
         —Hearn to Basil Hall Chamberlain, 31 October 1893

Since for Hearn, as for most foreigners, Fuji made a great impression at first sight, an essay that deals with the shifting prospects of the mountain serves as a template for Hearn's Japanese career, which developed from an initial exuberance through painful recognition to recovered, if subdued, poetic vision. Here is Hearn's first extensive description of the sacred mountain in *Glimpses of Unfamiliar Japan:*

Beyond that semicircle of green hills rises a lofty range of serrated mountains, indigo silhouettes. And enormously high above the line of them towers an apparition indescribably lovely,—one solitary snowy cone, so filmily exquisite, so spiritually white, that but for its immemorially familiar outline, one would surely deem it a shape of cloud. Invisible its base remains, . . . only above the eternal snow-line its dreamy cone appears, seeming to hang, the ghost of a peak, between the luminous land and the luminous heaven,—the sacred and matchless mountain, Fujiyama.[10]

And here is Hearn closer to the mountain and distant from his first impressions:

Then the huge dead crater,—probably between a quarter of a mile and half-a-mile wide, but shallowed up to within three or four hundred feet of the verge by volcanic detritus,—a cavity horrible even in the tones of its yellow crumbling walls, streaked and stained with every hue of scorching. I perceive that the trail of straw sandals [footwear of Japanese pilgrims] ends *in* the crater. Some hideous over-hanging cusps of black lava—like the broken edges of a monstrous cicatrix—project on two sides several hundred feet above the opening; but I certainly shall not take the time to climb them. Yet these,—seen through the haze of a hundred miles,—through the soft illusion of blue spring-weather,—appear as the opening snowy petals of the bud of the sacred lotus! . . . [sic] No spot in this world can be more horrible, more atrociously dismal, than the cindered tip of the Lotus as you stand upon it.[11]

Much in this passage typifies Hearn's writing about Japan, and even, in a mechanical sense, his writing before he saw Japan. The (over)use of dashes and other fragmenting punctuation; the reliance on superfluous exclamation marks; the suggestive ellipses; the hyperbole: All these can be seen as characteristics—and for many readers irritating characteristics—of his writings. Mannerisms aside, the passage speaks of physical terror, of an immensity frightening instead of inspiring, of emotional bleakness read into and drawn from the imposing mountain. Earlier in the essay Hearn had described the colors of the mountain, greens and blues turning to

black,—charcoal black,—a frightful extinct heap of visible ashes and cinders and slaggy lava. . . . Most of the green has disappeared. Likewise all of the illusion. The tremendous naked black reality,—always becoming more sharply, more atrociously defined,—is a stupefaction, a nightmare. . . . [sic] Above—miles above—the snow patches glare and gleam against the blackness,—hideously. I think of a gleam of white teeth I once saw in a skull,—a woman's skull,—otherwise burnt to a sooty crisp.[12]

A kind of suffocating materiality that reminds him of past horrors, Fuji evidently takes him back to reporting days in Cincinnati. Hearn's sensational accounts of the infamous Tanyard murder, with its dead *man's* skull, described the mostly charred remains and imagined for his readers both the panic of the dying man and the progress of his disintegration. The account was lurid, overstated, and shockingly evocative:

> On lifting the lid a powerful and penetrating odor, strongly resembling the smell of burnt beef, yet heavier and fouler, filled the room and almost sickened the spectators. But the sight of the black remains was far more sickening. Laid upon the clean white lining of the coffin they rather resembled great shapeless lumps of half-burnt coal.[13]

"Fuji-no-Yama," like so much of Hearn's later writing, shapes the earlier passion for horror into something less violent while equally disturbing. In this case the mountain as a remote ideal alters dramatically with closer knowledge. Taking what for most people is an exhilarating if tiring ascent of the holy mountain, Hearn makes it into a soul-wrenching experience, as frightening to the senses as it is fatiguing to the legs and lungs. Fuji's relatively easy slopes emerge as monstrous impediments, almost diabolical in their opposition, a place of trial where destruction and chaos are inescapable, where unblemished promise deteriorates, and the eager self suffers from torpor and disenchantment.

Hearn also transforms the mountain into a hideous woman with long flanks and other graphic suggestions of a female body, whose apparent beauty reveals itself as that of a deluding whore. Hearn's association of ugliness with women is both disturbing and predictable—predictable because he usually finds images of women for any extreme emotion and rarely stops a description without fully exploiting its imagistic powers. Here, as elsewhere, what had seemed alluringly feminine becomes discomforting, alien. A spiritual pilgrimage bestows the opposite of the pilgrim's expectations, revealing to him (and even more to his readers) the weight of conflicting emotions.

It is only when Hearn can safely turn from the images around him that he can regain his veneration, allowing the panorama of the climbed mountain to redeem what the journey has thoroughly undone:

But the view—the view for a hundred leagues,—and the light of
the far faint dreamy world,—and the fairy vapors of morning,—
and the marvelous wreathings of cloud: all this, and only this,
consoles me for the labor and the pain. . . . The immense poetry
of the moment enters into me with a thrill. I know that the
colossal vision before me has already become a memory
ineffaceable,—a memory of which no luminous detail can fade
till the hour when thought itself must fade, and the dust of these
eyes be mingled with the dust of the myriad million eyes that also
have looked, in ages forgotten before my birth, from the summit
supreme of Fuji to the Rising of the Sun.[14]

Much as for his favorite poet, Shelley, in "Mont Blanc,"
Hearn wills an inner concord only by distancing himself
from the mountain. The inflated and abstract rhetoric of
this hymn to Fuji implies not so much an Eastern apotheo-
sis but a Western assertion of the whole personality, or ego,
which Hearn theoretically rejects. Instead of a hoped for
salvation, the experience leads to an increasingly divided
sense of who he is.

Thoughts about "myriad million eyes" (not one of
Hearn's happiest phrases) point to his obsessive interest in
the workings, or at least the implications, of memory,
which complicate his viewpoint—and which long pre-
ceded his journey to Japan. An article for the New Orleans
Item told of a perhaps imaginary conversation between a
wandering dreamer and a practical doctor of medicine. It is
the doctor who shows the wanderer how his recurrent
dream of India reverts to his father's years in the subconti-
nent, now manifest in the son's inherited images. Whether
Hearn had his own father's experience in mind, he once
again points to archetypal memories connected with the
Orient, even at this time with the sensuous Orient of contemporary myth. In a different spirit, he combines an
awareness of Eastern religious traditions with what he
thinks of as scientific exploration and what was in fact
current discussion in psychological inquiries of the time.
Metempsychosis, the doctor suggests, is nothing more
than inherited memories of the sort Western speculators

were trying to define. Hence, while the wanderer's life touches the exotic, it parallels the lives of others who have never left the suburbs of New Orleans.

The various essays in *Exotics and Retrospectives* make clear the evolution of Hearn's ideas in Japan. Above all he seeks to explain the connection between theories of memory and his understanding of beauty, which is, he says, attributable to memory and to the divergent personalities that make up memory. When we see a beautiful face, we assess it through the eyes, in a sense, of our multitudes of ancestors who have looked and learned before us. Our fears as well as desires are governed by the composite selves of history. How else, he says, can we know when to be afraid, whom to trust, indeed how to respond to any sort of new experience? Originally drawing his theory from Herbert Spencer, whose insistence on "inherited characteristics" was meant to explain immediate generational inheritance of learned behavior that then became an automatic, or "unconscious," part of our functioning lives, Hearn tempered Spencer with Shinto belief in the survival of ancestors and Buddhist belief in the continuity of life.

Hearn seems untroubled by the paradoxical vision equating his Western perception with a collective Eastern past, as if he is the Western representative adopted by the East. He implies that through a trial like the climb of Fuji he has somehow identified with those myriad spirits he imagines to have ascended the mountain before him. The uncanny association haunts Hearn's vision of landscape or of self in landscape in an almost literal way. The ghosts of those we follow are within, determining our sense of what Carl Jung would call "synchronicity" and enriching the meanings of either pleasurable or terrifying experience. Hearn, however, turns such meaning inside out. The person who experiences horror, as Hearn so often did, actually experiences a breakdown of self—into those specters who are his past and personality. Indeed, horror or fear seems to generate the awareness of the ghosts, whose main effect is the destruction of personality. If Hearn can sometimes identify this breakdown with a positive acceptance of Buddhistic teachings, the rational explanation apparently offers minimal salve for his confused ego, what he accepts as his Western state of mind.

In a sense, Hearn's grasp of landscape seems no more a reflection of Buddhistic thinking than a reversion to nineteenth-century Western theories of the sublime, in which fear and awe compete with a gentler concept of beauty. For the Fuji essay is, in origin, topographical writing, which emphasizes shapes, rock configurations, sky color, temperature, sounds. All of Hearn's essays concentrate on physical qualities, whether the sound of *semi* (cicadas), the shapes of buildings, the angle of a woman's head, or the dustiness of a road in the heat of the day. When he tells of O kami, the seamstress, whose child's head is ripped off by an angry spirit, he evokes the darkness into which she goes, as if to live through with the reader the young woman's agonizing journey. In telling of a peasant on the bridge, he allows the reader a glimpse of the samurai who murdered enemy soldiers passing by, his perspective that of the trapped, bewildered man. A simple prototype of the writer himself, the peasant has never before told of his experience; his frightening encounter has instilled in him an awareness of a meaningful though alien sense of honor.

Whatever his topic, Hearn immerses himself in the scene described, hearing, seeing, smelling, touching. His praise of Walter Pater's ability to depict "fine and subtle and penetrating needle points of truth" speaks to his own practice and certainly to his ambitions, because he, too, as a writer of impressions, dedicates himself to the exact sensation and its precise verbal equivalent.[15] He recommends models in Japanese painting, which doubtless reinforced his notions of suggestiveness and impression, but, as his lectures on English writers suggest, Pater and late nineteenth-century followers of Pater had already shaped Hearn's aesthetic ideals.

For all his emphasis on impressions, Hearn's writing aspires to something quite different. Listening to his favorite words—words like *weird, ghostly, luminous, wonder, revery*—is to recognize his aspirations for more than what he writes or what he seems confident to understand. In "Fuji-no-Yama," as in other essays, Hearn emphasizes not merely the demoniacal essence of the mountain, its profound lights and darkness, and its sometimes overwhelming emptiness but also its increasingly phantasmagoric qualities. The rocks he dislodges in his clumsiness vanish without noise, giving him "a sensation like the sensation of falling in dreams."[16] As self changes or merges with the landscape, from which it draws contours and moods, he himself becomes the object he describes, and all objects take shape in a world of dreams.

The dreamlike quality in Hearn's vision of Japan captures the exotic nature of the land as he sees it and his own disappointed sense of the life he has chosen. "I have been," he says, "so disappointed."[17] Yet the process of the climb, the immersion into the radically disrupting experience, is what he seeks out *and* what he should expect to find. His repeated claims for divided personality, even for the lack of personality, in himself and others suggest that experiences like the climb of Fuji establish another order of self. Granting personality to be a fiction dependent on custom and delusion, something as intrinsically spiritual (in the eyes of Japanese) as the climb of a holy mountain would obviously threaten and disrupt. More than this, Hearn's ascent reduces him to a kind of abjectness, as if he has sunk emotionally as high as he has climbed physically, and the abjectness intersects with fear.[18] Fear dominates this essay: fear of the unknown, fear of heights, fear of falling, fear of disgracing himself, fear for others (such as a meteorologist and his wife who have tried, without heat, to survive the long winter on the summit of the mountain). Fear involves, at last, fear of death, and while Hearn may argue for the continuity of spirit and the essential meaninglessness of death, awareness of death haunts his lived and his written experiences.

For Lafcadio Hearn, complicated relationships between

fear, beauty, and dreams focus repeatedly on issues of space. The man who spent almost all of his time in the last years of his life in the safety of his own study was a man troubled by open places as well as jaded by what he had formerly cherished. As a young man, Hearn described being hoisted up the steeple of St. Peter's Cathedral in Cincinnati.[19] The story may be apocryphal, and in any case begs a few questions, since, given his poor eyesight, Hearn could probably have seen little from the top of the church—any more, presumably, than he could have seen from the summit of Fuji. Whatever the truth of the steeple anecdote, seeking out and writing about unusual places had been habitual to Hearn, who loved to swim far out to sea or find the most isolated of religious shrines, describing himself in such places or situating his characters there. The climb of Fuji was another act of pride or defiance, the more so for someone whose flawed sight translated the unseen into the threatening. Its effect on the climber involves an odd reversal of space and self, "height growing above depth,"[20] the zigzag way engulfing the weary and disturbed acolyte. Hearn's more beautiful prospect, the early morning sun and the rolling clouds at the mountain's summit, appears as a vision of the sea, which reassures or reinvites the lost calm. Open space troubled Hearn less when he saw it in terms of the ocean he loved.

In much of Hearn's writing about Japan the pattern of the Fuji essay is more or less reversed, with comfortable space succeeding to threatening space, as it did in Hearn's retreat to the sanctity of his writing room. On his arrival in Yokohama, as he describes in *Glimpses*, Hearn had found the daintiest of shops, the most diminutive of streets, the most peculiar of shrines. Like Dickens on cozy interiors, he seems fascinated by enclosed places, which he sees, in contrast to the obviously sexual threat of Fuji, as feminine but maternal. Such privileged space is as important to Hearn as "sublime" space, for which it is a counter or possibly an escape. To see Hearn moving in his writings from the one to the other helps to indicate some of the emotional tug-of-war in the essays he writes. After an arduous walk he recovers in the peaceful twilight of a graveyard; from a boat ride along a rocky coast he sails into the capacious but enclosed and satisfying space of a cave/shrine. From the streets of Yokohama he enters the darkness of a Shinto shrine, in the darkest corner of which is a statue or, with an irony he appreciates, a mirror. (Without developing differences between Western and Eastern responses to mirrors as signs, Hearn anticipates Jacques Lacan, Tzvetan Todorov, and recent critics, who emphasize that the recognition of self comes through confrontation with an other, even when the other appears as one's own reflected image.)

Enclosed and pleasing spaces are not, of course, Hearn's personal property. For Gaston Bachelard they underlie a phenomenological process Bachelard sees as a crucial image-making function and the basis for what amounts to an aesthetics of self.[21] Hearn's constant presentation of spatial images, whether in landscape or interiors, would be an index of his poetic capacities, his imaginative making or remaking of spaces from memory, his proving of a basic writing gift. Bachelard scarcely mentions the relationship of one image to another, except as a key to "the poetics of space," and a given poet might be unable to write more than a series of images and still excel as an imaginative writer. Hearn himself rarely sustains his essay-reveries, which are almost always alive with powerful images while apparently unfinished as sustained work. He polishes loosely connected fragments, leaving the whole to be interpreted by his reader.

3   Buddhism in some form will exist after Christianity and Christian religions have vanished. The argument must be based first of all upon the enormous cost of individuation in the West. . . .
    —Hearn to Basil Hall Chamberlain, 28 April 1893

The process of the Fuji essay follows a typical pattern, as if the more rarefied the situation the more extreme Hearn's thinking, which escapes from ordinary boundaries and reaches farther than the writer himself had dared to imagine. The process need not result from a dramatic journey. An essay called "In Yokohama," a part of the collection *Out of the East*, moves quietly toward the same end. Here Hearn describes a visit five years before to a small Jizo temple where he had met a wise old priest. The story breaks into two complementary parts, the first reporting his conversations with the priest, the second, on his return, with the priest's successor, for the old priest has in the meantime died. In a more deliberate, more intellectual way Hearn uses the two episodes to explore the same kinds of topics as in the Fuji essay, except that "In Yokohama" takes an interrogative form, one question following another, so that narrative remains incidental and struggle for understanding less physical.

"In Yokohama" may remind us how much of Hearn's work asks questions and how appropriate questions are as a reflection of his life in Japan. Anecdotal and chatty, the essay begins with Hearn looking for the temple, which, typically, "was not easy to find, being hidden away in a court behind a street of small shops." The brief search for the place itself promises the search for what it means or what answers it might provide. Odd and unimposing, with Western jars and cigarette boxes prominently on display, the temple offers things "unseen." Its priest is an unassuming man, "very pleasant to look upon," wrinkled and kind. "His voice was deep and gentle," resembling (and this is Hearn's highest praise) the rich sounds of a bronze bell. According to his successor, the priest has wasted his years writing a voluminous religious history of Japan, "full of impossible stories—miracles and fairy tales." The young man's contempt applies, implicitly, to Hearn himself, who might have described his own account of Japan (and perhaps does) with precisely these words: "impossible

stories—miracles and fairy tales."22 Like the old priest, he
is at once undisciplined and continually searching, aware
that formulated questions are both necessary and puerile,
that they merely touch life's deepest enigmas.

As Marcel Robert pointed out (in his little known but
illuminating biography), Hearn combined the qualities of
an aggressive journalist with those of a sympathetic lis-
tener, almost forcing his entry as the first Westerner into a
variety of Japanese sanctuaries then exploiting his shyness
to open others to his questions.23 In this episode, after
Hearn's humble courtesies, the old priest speaks relatively
freely and generously to his Western guest. The opportunity prompts Hearn to a litany of questions: "Are all our
bodily weaknesses and misfortunes . . . the results of errors committed in other births?" "Can a man obtain the
power to remember his former births?" The priest answers
patiently, while Hearn's thoughts expand beyond simple
questions and answers. He notices the priest's "red cat,"
remarks on new guests entering the temple, then moves on
to long reveries: "Involuntarily there came to me the idea
of all the countless innocent prayers thus being made in
countless temples." After fleeting thoughts about a universe beyond comprehension, even with the Buddhist medium, his concentration returns to the temple then once
again to the priest and his own concerns:

A little silence followed,—softly broken by the purring of the cat.
I looked at the picture of Adelaide Neilson [a Victorian actress
who died young and was famous for her Juliet] just visible above
the top of the screen; and I thought of Juliet, and wondered what
the priest would say about Shakespeare's wondrous story of passion and sorrow, were I able to relate it worthily in Japanese. Then
suddenly, like an answer to that wonder, came a memory of the
two hundred and fifteenth verse of the Dhamma-pada: *"From
love comes grief; from grief comes fear: one who is free from love
knows neither grief nor fear."*

"Does Buddhism," I asked, "teach that all sexual love ought to
be suppressed?"24

Here, for one of the few times in his public writings, Hearn confronts what obviously preoccupied him in his private thinking, as if he finally separates lust and friendship, or learns to connect lust with grief and fear.[25] When he has voiced his most difficult conundrums, Hearn slips back into revery, contemplating his own questions and the priest's wise and necessarily inadequate replies, until it is time to leave.

The second part of the essay, beginning once again with a search for the temple, offers a kind of Wordsworthian recollection. Hearn speaks of returning after five years, five long years, during which he has lost the "beautiful illusion" of Japan. With his recurrent metaphor of journey, Hearn had asked the priest an indirect question—distinctly not Wordsworthian—about the progress of life in relation to bodily things: "I cannot help thinking that the way of progress must continually grow more difficult the further one proceeds. For . . . the more one succeeds in detaching one's self from the things of the senses the more powerful become the temptations to return to them."[26] The sad, deeply personal revelation emphasizes a kind of eternal return, which mocks both earthly life and its aspirations for ascetic discipline. *Return* is the key word in describing Hearn's thinking and the direction of his essays.

Return to the reliance on the sensual or sensible world is maybe unavoidable for a man whose writing had always emphasized the physical, insisting on sensual impressions, and creating for and with readers the illusion of being in the place described. Return here means, as it usually does for Hearn, something much larger and more complex—witness his original sense of "return" to Japan itself—yet it begins with the simple physical return to the temple. One profound difference between the two visits can only be clear to the reader of the earlier account, which describes Hearn's coming to the temple with Akim, his first guide in Japan. Without Akim he has, almost literally, lost both ears and tongue, for Akim (a young priest at the

time of Hearn's arrival in Japan) led him to such sanctuaries and served as translator and interpreter. Revisiting
the temple unaccompanied by his guide, he seeks a further
message from the dead priest aside from the mechanics of
Buddhist theology. He hopes to find meaning in his exiled
life. Like the ascent of Fuji, this return forces him to con-
template what his tourist self had never needed to recognize: "I began to think the unthinkable."[27]

The unthinkable involves that which cannot, consciously, be formulated—to learn from the priest's
lesson—and means essentially the "unity of life," something so vast as to be unthinkable, in his own words, and
vast enough to dwarf the sensual and self-consciously frail
person who thinks. Imagined unity of life offers in a certain
sense grounds for reassurance, because continuing life
means a victory over physical death. "If the ghost in each
one of us must have passed through the burning of a million suns," however, the survival of memory in our own
small ghost can hardly be of great comfort. Brave questioning aside, comfort is what Hearn needs: "I have searched
Buddhist books for answers to these questions, and I found
answers which seemed to me better than any others. Still,
they did not satisfy me."[28] The return to the priest for
possible answers meets with the same result, which is,
ironically, the emptiness, or at least the absence of answers, that the priest's religion ultimately promises.

It is as if each of Hearn's experiences in Japan—whether
on a mountaintop or within a temple—recapitulates his
entire Japanese experience. Not only has this man "learned
to see the Far East without its glamour,"[29] he has been
forced to see himself comparably diminished. Like so
many Westerners before and after him, seeking a kind of
Nirvana while finally incapable of its ascetic trials, Hearn
keeps returning to where he began. Perhaps his only progress is a growing rejection of the world around him, the
rejection not so much for the end of contemplation or
ultimate renunciation as for escape and solitude, for the

opportunity to write more about what the man honestly confesses he understands less.

Both the essay on Fuji and "In Yokohama" recount meetings with people—the mountain guides, the old priest—while subtly emphasizing the aloneness of the person writing. In a fascinating study of solitude, subtitled "A Return to the Self," the psychoanalyst Anthony Storr argues against conventional notions of close personal relations as foundations for happiness or creative lives. He calls his discussion a response to what have become post-Freudian norms of behavior, although he seems also to revert to nineteenth-century ideas about the lonely and exiled artist lost in a world that neither understands nor cares.[30] Storr suggests that many people, and certainly many artists, can function perfectly well in solitude, which may be a necessary condition for their work.

Lafcadio Hearn offers a good example of Storr's solitary artist, although he gives the lie to any constraining or absolute theory about human personality. Sometimes, that is, he needed people desperately; sometimes he avoided people as if they were meddling with his soul. It is true that Hearn argued, overtly or tacitly, the need for family and family ties. He could embarrass acquaintances by interrogating jinrikisha men about the love they had for their wives: "Do you love your wife?"[31] As if his business would not extend to someone who said no. As if, too, his own earlier life had been a model of passionate commitment or focused sexuality. Clearly, Hearn loved his children, especially Kazuo, the firstborn child he mentions so often and with such feeling in letters to Elizabeth Bisland. Yet Hearn's lifelong pattern of new beginnings points to an alternative set of values, to the need for solitary experiences and separation from others. I am not speculating about the "normalcy" of his behavior, any more than about its health. Hearn's escapes *were* escapes and not solely his desire for a new start or for personal autonomy. He was running away more typically than running toward any definite goal or ideal. Seeking out the remote, the singular, the solitary, Hearn found in Japan mirror images of his own lonely self.

For all his interest in people, Hearn records what are nonetheless solitary experiences or seeks in others the accounts of their solitary experiences, whether a woman speaking to her own diary, an idiosyncratic priest, or a principled man set apart by generosity and strength. These individuals serve as emblems of human dignity or tragedy, their entire inner lives posited from outer, public conduct. Hearn is profoundly sympathetic without presuming to know other psyches.

One reason for Hearn's distance from the solitaries he describes is language, or what amounted to his failure of language in a foreign land. Try as he did—with endless lists and questions—Hearn could not master Japanese. Although his power with his native language may well have increased with the struggle, he could never replace Akim with his own command of Japanese. Those countless vagrants, barbers, slaughterhouse workers, and police officers whom he described in his journalism days were people he could listen to, whose language (or dialect) he could learn, and that was no less true of the Creoles in New Orleans or Martinique. The representative characters he describes in Japan are isolated from him as he remained isolated from the people he met.

Hearn's incapacity to become fluent in Japanese seems fitting for someone who saw himself as set apart, deaf to the meanings of foreign words, let alone to nuance of intonation, condemned to an exile's silence. Perhaps nothing isolates like the inability to hear and understand the language of a country in which one lives, the more so when that country's life and culture provide the focus of one's writing. It might be said that Hearn lived in Japan like a deaf person, with some of the consequent loneliness of the disability. He writes *as if* part of his retraction from society might have resulted from problems of hearing and language learning, which must have been all the more troubling for a man who had been such a linguist early in his years. (The analogy might be with a composer such as the older Beethoven, unable to hear his music, except in the interior of his own brain.) Rejection of friends would provide another index of the separation felt by a deaf person, who would rather avoid the pain of not hearing than inflict his incapacity on friends.

From neither Hearn nor his family, however, is there a hint about deafness. He goes into great detail about "insect musicians," as he calls them, or the sounds of Japanese instruments, or he describes with care the singing of a blind beggar near his house; obviously, he retained his hearing, continuing his interest in the quality of sounds— voices, noises, musical instruments—that characterized his writings in Cincinnati. As a friend of the musicologist Henry Krehbiel, Hearn collected songs, studied dialects, and served even in those years as a kind of amateur musician, and in Japan, according to his wife, he remained exceedingly sensitive to any sound. What happened may have been something comparable to deafness, perhaps a sort of deafness to other people, to anyone or anything that interfered with the necessary isolation for writing. "Nor is there singing school" for the writer's soul, as William Butler Yeats wrote, "but studying monuments of its own magnificence."[32]

4   Is it not proper to say that Mr. Hearn has introduced a
new element of psychology into literature?
—Paul Elmer More, "Lafcadio Hearn"

Hearn's increasing preoccupation with Buddhist thought and its relation to his own life continues in an 1899 collection, *In Ghostly Japan*. The book opens with "A Fragment," a dream that tells of a religious aspirant climbing a mountain of skulls, the detritus of his own former selves, which Hearn describes, like the climb of Fuji, as an excursion into fear and loathing. The language combines Buddhist sutras and Ezekiel (with echoes of Dante):

And it was at the hour of sunset that they came [the acolyte and his Virgil-like guide] to the foot of the mountain. There was in that place no sign of life,—neither token of water, nor trace of plant, nor shadow of flying bird,—nothing but desolation rising to desolation.[33]

Much of *Ghostly Japan* explores metaphysical problems, either narratively or essayistically, posing questions about the hollowness of life or the meaning of death. Whether talking about the mountain of skulls, incense, "A Story of Divination," or directly about "Japanese Buddhist Proverbs," Hearn meditates, writing for his Western audience in his recognizable way yet writing intently about Eastern religious issues. To categorize this man as a translator from the Japanese (which he was not), as a simple purveyor of Japanese culture to the West, or as a folklorist addicted to old legends means ignoring his increasingly spiritual exercises and their effect on the unassuming power of his writing. Yet even the word *spiritual* hardly touches the psychological complexities underlying Hearn's writing. In a passage that addresses both his writing process and its implications, he says: "*Unconscious* brain-work is the best to develop . . . latent feeling or thought. By quietly writing the thing over and over again, I find that the emotion or idea often *develops itself* in the process,—unconsciously. Again, it is often worthwhile to *try* to analyze the feeling that remains dim." Anticipating Maurice Merleau-Ponty and other commentators on the writing process, Hearn also explores what Freud and Jung were to contribute to depth psychology: "When the best result comes [in writing], it ought to surprise you, for our best work is out of the Unconscious."[34]

One essay from *Ghostly Japan* seems especially to explore the world of the unconscious and its relation to ancestral memory and Buddhism. It is an odd but exemplary tour de force. Instead of sights, it speaks of sounds, while turning again to problems of life and belief. "Ululation," like the Fuji essay, reaches back to articles written by Hearn earlier in his career, exploiting the macabre world that Hearn found so intriguing in writers like Poe or Baudelaire. It works as another sort of revery, a sometimes circular, or at least circuitous, reflection of a journey of the mind, except that here the traveler is, in William Blake's phrase, a "mental traveller," confronting eternity in his own backyard. A world of dreams, the space between a mundane and an unconscious world, is the realm of *Ghostly Japan* and other Japanese books in which revery dominates. "*Think not that dreams appear to the dreamer only at night: the dream of this world of pain appears to us even by day.*"[35]

Ululation, meaning "howling," "wailing," or "loud lamentation"—to use the sequence of synonyms from the *Oxford English Dictionary*—refers simply to Hearn's dog in Tokyo, which kept him awake at night with her haunting cries. Hearn makes of the howling a metaphysical contemplation, associating the dog with ancient memories and Buddhist thinking, while imagining the "primitive fears" and inner life of his wolflike creature. In turn, the imagined thoughts of the dog provide a way to make an oblique scrutiny of his own thoughts about existence, nonexistence, and the possibilities of a Buddhist Nirvana for the exiled soul.

The revery begins with unadorned description: "She is lean as a wolf, and very old,—the white bitch that guards my gate at night."[36] From details about her perilous life— she has barely escaped being put down as a homeless dog— Hearn goes on to describe her virtues, making them, as he often does with animals, resemble the human. Accepting an Eastern notion of the continuities of life and things, he credits the animal with deep, though unsophisticated, emotion.

"Curious-looking," if not actually ugly, the dog has somehow won his affection: "I have only one fault to find with her: she howls at night." It is the howling that disturbs him, profoundly disturbs him, so that the auditory supplants the visual. No mere sound or sounds, the howling becomes an echo and a signal, a grotesque music about the prospects of death:

It begins with a stifled moan, like the moan of a bad dream,—mounts into a long wail, like a wailing of wind,—sinks quavering into a chuckle,—rises again to a wail, very much higher and wilder than before,—breaks suddenly into a kind of atrocious laughter, and finally sobs itself out in a plaint like the crying of a little child.

The association of the wolflike dog with human beings and human sentiments leads Hearn to think of incongruity akin to madness. "Too savagely close to Nature" to mourn long for a dead human, the dog would, he imagines, mourn briefly her master's death before eating his corpse, "cracking his bones between those long wolf's-teeth of hers. And thereafter, with spotless conscience, she would sit down and utter to the moon the funeral cry of her ancestors." The paradox or incongruity may—who knows?—lie within the dog herself. But, manifestly, Hearn hears the savage music in response to his own feelings. "The whole thing is a song," along with the response of other dogs, distant and troubled, who perceive the "humanly unimaginable" while fully imagined implications of the painful lament.[37]

What the dog herself hears and sings about, Hearn suggests, is inherited fear, fear emanating from "things myriads of years old"—fear akin to the beauty on Mount Fuji or the troubling beauty he may see in a stranger's face. "Since the senses of a dog are totally unlike those of a man, we shall never really know [what its "dim inheritance" means]. And we can only surmise, in the vaguest way, the meaning of the uneasiness in ourselves. Some notes [nevertheless] oddly resemble those tones of the human voice that tell of agony and terror."[38] Coincidental as her sex may be, the bitch's power and fascination recall the female power ascribed to Mount Fuji and to the female characters in the ghost stories. Hearn came to think of Japan in its ghostly role, which provided him with a kind of psychic space or distance, at once closer to the meaning of what he experienced and farther from its everyday reality. If the highest gods were feminine in spirit, so were the most potent, perhaps the most demonic forces, which Hearn intuited from any number of unlikely sources. Like the howling dog and the blackened mountain, Japan becomes both a woman and a ghost, manageable in narrative but an other never fully to be assimilated.

When thinking about the dog's feelings, Hearn manages to project himself into an extraordinary state of mind, as if he *can* know that the dog's apprehension comes from smells not sight, from a range of being unfathomable to humans, though somehow parallel to that of humans, if not finally identical. The dog serves to reveal a wider sensibility, an apprehension of other meanings, all of which bear on the writer's own primitive and vulnerable self. This revery turns back time and again to human application, arguing, for example, that the wolf-dog's eating resembles our own, for whatever we eat, as vegetarians or carnivores, we inevitably kill what we devour; we *must* kill to survive. Hearn's moral may be crude, but he wants to demonstrate the folly of illusions, the impermanence of ordinary values; he wants to question (like his contemporaries Jack London and Joseph Conrad) the perilous state of society founded on primitive forces, which it chooses to deny: "The very speech of that Nature so inexplicably called by poets the loving, the merciful, the divine! Divine, perhaps in some unknowable ultimate way,—certainly not merciful, and still more certainly not loving."[39]

Hearn's echoes of Tennyson on "Nature red in tooth and claw" and of other Victorian students of evolution and uncertainty illuminate the background of some of these passages. Here is a late nineteenth-century writer disillusioned with inherited notions of culture, someone who refers to Matthew Arnold as "the colossal humbug of the century"[40] and who, like Thomas Hardy, for example, struggles for values in a world without beliefs.

This tells only part of the story. By the end of the century, Lafcadio Hearn is a man caught like the dog in "Ululation," not just between a dead world and another trying to be born but also between a dead world and an undiscoverable inner life. He knows the teachings of Buddha, as the episode about the priest and other direct "gleanings in Buddha-fields" make clear. At the same time, like the unconscious wolf-dog, he can only speak, or write, about problems. He cannot solve them. An uncertain or teasing form reflects a fretting and searching mind. Here, as in most of his writings, a revery leaps from personal observation and ordinary fact to exploration of another order, in which "horror" provides a kind of spiritual lens for the world he sees. Only a small part of that world remains the Japan described in the early writings; the rest emerges from the author's solitary meditation.

[4]
Spirits, Ghosts, and "Sundry Cobwebs"

1   The horror of the [ghost] story comes from the force
     with which it makes us realize the power that our
     minds possess for such excursions into the darkness.
                    —Virginia Woolf, "The Supernatural in Fiction"
                                                         (1918)

An essay such as "Fuji-no-Yama" raises many questions, and perhaps one above all. If, to indulge in one of the favorite metaphors of his age, Hearn could put on the clothes of his new culture, could he to his own satisfaction internalize its voice? The howl of the tormented dog, its ululation haunting his nights and reminding him of memories neither canine nor human—or, rather, both in some estranging state of revery—suggests that no public articulation offers full correspondence for private suffering. The dog's wild cries "speak" to Hearn's own isolation in a society the language of which remains foreign and, like the dog's, essentially unspeakable. Does Hearn even want the risk of internalizing a language he comes increasingly to recognize as alien, at least if the implied cost of a chosen identity means the loss of a known identity? Is this the anguish for him in the dog's cry, the frustration at not finding answers from the dead Buddhist priest, the horror—like Kurtz's staggering horror in *Heart of Darkness*—felt on the climb of Fuji? The circular, self-surprising development of the reveries presents an emblem of Japan's adopted son ever in the process of filling in or shading or hiding a frightening interior.

The indeterminate structure of the reveries, however much it reflects the movements of actual daydream or associative thinking, allows the retention of a public persona and a private train of thought, one more confessional and intimate than the revery actually becomes—or its author allows. For the assembled sections, or fragments, reveal different roles: the would-be Buddhist, the sympathetic historian, the gentleman naturalist, the cultural minister, the translator, the literary interpreter, the philosopher, almost at times the Whitmanesque explorer of an unbounded self-in-multitude. Hearn's stylistic roles are many. If he controls them, it is more by balance than integration, more by parallels than form, with form construed in his sense of tightly ordered and crafted language. Hearn's writings disregard the kinds of rigorous design he often demands of other writers' work in his critical essays. Instead, they are essays in the original sense of trials and explorations, tentative gropings toward truth often too terrible to encounter. In an article about the horror of Gothic architecture in *Shadowings* (1900), he assumes the safe perspective of a child looking with fear at the "power" of Gothic forms, but it is his own controlled terror he reveals:

To his startled imagination, the building stretches itself like a phantasm of sleep,—makes itself tall and taller with intent to frighten. Even though built by hands of men, it has ceased to be a mass of dead stone: it is infused with Something that thinks and threatens;—it has become a shadowing malevolence, a multiple goblinry, a monstrous fetish![1]

Hearn's ghost stories perhaps offered a way of presenting such disquieting thoughts while avoiding the imminence of personal destruction he struggles against in "Fuji-no-Yama." Without the autobiographical format of the reveries, his ghost stories dramatize the personal as collective or racial powers, part of a larger metaphysic of good and evil, which he can integrate in the framework of narrative. His fascination with Japanese ghost stories (*kwaidan*, or *kaidan*) grew out of a lifelong interest in the supernatural, in the ways that ordinary experience intersects with a complex realm of indefinable forces and interrelationships.

To explore the psychology of ghost stories meant exploring an unknown world, as if, like Urashima, Hearn submerged himself below the surface of an unplumbed sea. Ghost stories allowed a measure of control over personal doubt and desire, involving at once a lowering of boundaries of self and the erection of more concrete barriers. To reconstruct Japanese ghost stories was, to put this differently, a way of reaching the supernatural or the uncanny, or both, through acceptable and often ancient accounts, in which the personal is both subordinate and paramount, its inmost fears realized with the least of risks. This is what Freud would soon be saying about writers and their daydreaming (reveries, as Hearn would say) and about the play of the unconscious in literary works.[2]

A self-styled "psychological" reader of fiction, although too early to read Freud (*The Interpretation of Dreams* appeared in 1900, four years before his death), Hearn shared with his English and American contemporaries a profound interest in supernatural fiction. Hearn's own generation, in England as well as America, wrote prolifically about the supernatural. This was, arguably, the great age of the ghost story. What might be called ghost-stories-of-manners in Henry James or Edith Wharton, near ghost stories (stories of madness and psychological extremes) in Charlotte Perkins Gilman's "Yellow Wallpaper," or "weird" stories of fate and fatal irony in Ambrose Bierce won great popularity in the late nineteenth and early twentieth centuries. Kipling, another well-known writer who experimented with ghost stories, seemed to Hearn to be a master of the supernatural. One of his many tributes to Kipling takes a typically exclamatory turn: "What complexities of suffering, of knowledge, of penetration, of tolerance . . . and all diabolical intuition are summed up in that one young life. What a revelation of the ghostliness of matter."[3] It was precisely his perception of "the ghostliness of matter" that defined Hearn's mature writings and focused his response to other writers.

Hearn remained throughout his adult life a passionate apologist for an early idol, Edgar Allan Poe, whose radical sensibilities seemed akin to his own. Poe represented a fictional world more profoundly interesting than that of other American writers, although Nathaniel Hawthorne's tales also appealed to him. I shall speak about Hearn's readings of Poe in the following chapter. What he emphasizes in Poe is less the narrative skill than the emotional effects of the tales, or the psychological conditions in which they flourish. "A little of the element of fear enters into every great and noble emotion," he says, "and especially into the higher forms of aesthetic feeling." If Poe's "nightmare absolute," or his depiction of the "atrociously ugly," is singular in depth or intensity, all nightmares in literature, Poe's included, demand "a clever mixture of the playful and the terrible."[4]

Hearn often framed his readings of other writers in terms of grotesque power, arguing, for instance, Zola's underrated strength as a creator of stunning effects, an impresario of the preternatural: "If there is anything," he writes to Chamberlain, "that Zola is not—it is a realist. His mind conceives the horrible as [Gustave] Doré's mind conceived the ghastly and the nightmarish. He is the idealist of the Horrible, the Foul, the Brutal, the Abominable."[5] Hearn's admiration for other French writers, especially Baudelaire, speaks to his obsession with things either sensually exotic or unreachably distant, and he finds Baudelaire's vision to be directly related, as well as indebted, to that of Poe. Hearn reads Poe, Baudelaire, and Zola as writers trespassing over boundaries of consciousness, mixing in their equally shocking ways a frightening prospect of inner and outer truth. Symbolist poet or naturalist or pseudoscientific novelist come together to shape literary directions (although Hearn thought modern literature, on the whole, to be in a sorry state). When the novelist William Dean Howells reviewed *Youma* he described

Hearn's own work as a kind of realism derived from the exotic, understanding Hearn as Hearn himself understood Baudelaire or Zola.[6] One singular characteristic did not isolate an author from his contemporaries, and Hearn could be read as both an independent and a representative writer.

While Hearn rarely mentions British ghost stories—by Sheridan Le Fanu and other masters of the genre—he remained intrigued by any writing—literary, religious, or philosophical—that probed dangerous regions of the mind. His exposure of the practitioners of "spirit photography" in Cincinnati came only after sympathetic appreciation of the scientific conmanship used by the photographers and after considerable desire on Hearn's part that the dead just might reveal themselves on the shadowy and suggestive plates sold to eager customers. Again the insistence on organic memory, which he associates with the technology of developing photographic images, reflects his conviction that there are indeed beings among and within us whose presence warrants attention.

He makes this point directly in a piece titled "A Ghost," written for *Harper's Magazine* in 1889, shortly before his departure for Japan. Defining his own life and the consequences of its "nomadic" course, he sees a kind of elective affinity between a wanderer like himself and the ghosts he will meet:

Perhaps the man who never wanders away from the place of his birth may pass all his life without knowing ghosts; but the nomad is more than likely to make their acquaintance. I refer to the civilized nomad, whose wanderings are not prompted by the hope of gain, nor determined by pleasure, but simply controlled by certain necessities of his being,—the man whose inner secret nature is totally at variance with the stable conditions of a society to which he belongs only by accident.[7]

Hearn would soon test his inner secrets against the conditions, stable or otherwise, of yet another society. This civilized nomad brought his ghosts to Japan and encountered new ones, except that here the wanderer and the so-

ciety as a whole shared a supernatural acquaintance. Belonging "only by accident" in this society, Hearn continued to discover his own ghosts, as his prophecy anticipated, for, while he found some contentment in Japan
along with new materials for his writings, he remained at
the least a mental wanderer and, in his own words, a ghost
himself.

2   I have the double sensation of being myself a ghost
         and of being haunted,—haunted by the prodigious
         luminous Spectre of the World.
                                               —Hearn, "Dust"

Hearn had believed in ghosts from the days when Sarah
Brenane locked him in the unlit rooms of her unfriendly
house, forcing the sensitive boy to imagine a frightening
region of spiritual tormentors: "For the best of possible
reasons I then believed in ghosts and in goblins—because I
saw them, both by day and by night."[8] Notwithstanding
his admiration for the clear answers of Herbert Spencer, he
was drawn to the irrational and the inexplicable—and, in a
broader sense, to what Spencer himself conceded and
Hearn repeated as the "Unknowable," that which defeated
even Spencer's arbitrary explanations. Personal no less
than collective (he might have said archetypal) images are,
in Hearn's words, invariably ghostly, with the result that
throughout his writings experiences from the banal to the
sublime elicit the same sort of image or metaphor. Speaking at one point about the exquisite beauty of a child's
calligraphy, he says that "it was not the beauty of the thing
in itself which impressed me, but the weird, extraordinary,
indubitable proof it afforded of an inherited memory. . . .
The thing was never the work of an individual child five
years old, but beyond all question the work of ghosts,—the
countless ghosts that make the compound ancestral
soul."[9] Art, in other words, no less than other civilized
activities, emerges from the unconscious realm of ghostly

recollection; it speaks to a kind of community in the shared creation of beauty.

Just how much value actual ghosts retained for Hearn can be seen in *Japan*, where he shows how family ghosts (ancestors in the Shinto faith) determine the shape of Japanese civilization. The history of Japan is in essence the history of her religion, her civilization its living dead.

No single fact in this connection is more significant than the fact that the ancient Japanese term for government—"matsuri-goto"—signifies literally "matters of worship." Later on we shall find that not only government, but almost everything in Japanese society, derives directly or indirectly from this ancestor-cult; and that in all matters the dead, rather than the living, have been the rulers of the nation and the shapers of its destiny.[10]

Hearn may have been mistaken in thinking that Eastern philosophy and Spencer could be wedded together satisfactorily, although he pointed repeatedly to Spencer's conviction that ancestor worship underlay all religious development, Eastern or Western. He did not err in finding Japanese mythology and art congruent with his belief in the supernatural. What he discovered in Japan was a world of the supernatural even more extensive than that in the West, a world that fitted happily with a still untrammeled natural beauty and with his own interests. Throughout the Edo period (1600–1867), development of grotesque and violent effects in popular literature meant a large public consciousness of ghosts and supernatural matters, which epitomized both the social state of the country and its religious traditions.[11] From the eighth century, when the stories in the *Nihongi* were collected, the supernatural had played an important part in Japanese legends, and no era had been without its interest in the frightening and grotesque. Perhaps the instability of the late Edo years had helped to increase public interest in "grotesqueries," as James A. Michener has called them.[12]

Certainly the theater was full of ghostly returns, bloody vengeance, and terrible ordeals. The nonaristocratic art of ukiyo-e, often depicting actors and scenes from Kabuki, focused on similar topics, most of which Hearn attended to or used for his own ends.[13] Katsushika Hokusai became one of Hearn's favorite artists, and Hokusai's *Manga* ("random sketches" or "cartoons") is full of grotesque representations. It is worth remembering that, for Hearn, Hokusai stood as a true artist, unencumbered by excessive detail and all the more authentic for his suggestive methods.[14] Hearn argued with English reviewers and the Japanese ambassador to England about the importance of ukiyo-e artists, Hokusai foremost among them.

Late Edo and Meiji Japanese emphasis on the grotesque managed to fit with traditional Buddhist thinking. Although the sutras and the exorcizing powers of priests were considered potent against supernatural evils, Buddhist ideas of hell had enriched Japanese storytelling over the centuries.[15] Terrifying notions of hell aside, spirits of the dead in Buddhist thinking made their way to a final eternity through an intermediate, almost purgatorial realm wherein things could go badly. Improper action by survivors might lure unhappy spirits back again to haunt households and do mischief—and provide material for marvelously diverse storytelling.

Drawing on a wide range of popular materials for his stories—as, for example, those in *Kwaidan*—Hearn describes the spirits of women returning to destroy incriminating love letters or spirits of abandoned wives returning to make love with their grief-stricken and easily deceived husbands, who usually wake up to misery and empty skeletons the morning after. The dead play prominent roles in many of Hearn's Japanese writings. Jealous ex-wives punish the wives taken by their husbands or assume unlikely shapes (as insects, for example) to warn the living of unfinished business. Hearn's range of interest extends from simple horror stories to narratives about delicate relationships, the kind of subtle connections between the living and the dead that Vladimir Nabokov wrote about in his novels, in which the dead touch the living in solicitous, if attenuated, ways.[16]

It might be said that all Hearn's Japanese books aspire to the condition of ghost stories, whether they introduce discussions of religious belief or give accounts of ghostly visitations. Even Hearn's early writings had tended to take ordinary experience into a realm of the bizarre and grotesque, so much so that an article about, say, a slaughterhouse could read like a report from hell, or a description of a policeman's rounds on the waterfront could suggest a disquieting confrontation with alien souls. Brilliantly described, Cincinnati becomes "the city of dreadful night," the original of which Hearn admired so much in the poet James Thompson. Hearn's emphasis on the exotic nature of Martinique or the "gruesome" qualities of Cincinnati may be written with "colloquial ease" and "idiomatic purity,"[17] yet he rarely writes for long without the hyperbole of *atrocious* or *ghastly* or some other word suggestive of extremity. This is true even though his Japanese writings remain, on balance, more controlled than the earlier works. In a sense, whether spare or florid, the effect is similar, because Hearn habitually insinuates a sphere of the uncanny, unexplored, and vaguely troubling.

Japan offered Hearn supernatural material without the need for radical readjustments. One of his pre-Japanese publications, *Some Chinese Ghosts* (1887), attests to his early interest in Oriental topics, which already included folklore and the study of Eastern religions.[18] The stories in *Chinese Ghosts* resemble in format those written about comparable materials in Japan, and appropriately so, since Japanese storytellers had borrowed over the centuries from the Chinese; but "the Japanese story-teller," as Hearn says, "has so recolored and reshaped his borrowing as to naturalize it."[19] Like another early volume, *Stray Leaves from Strange Literatures* (1884),[20] *Chinese Ghosts* gathers up assorted stories, lumping them together without apparent order or logic. Despite Hearn's request of Chamberlain to read this book as at most a crude index of things to come, his emphasis could have been on continuity, on the "reshaping" and "naturalizing" of materials that prefigured the writing in Japan. The young woman who throws herself into the molten metals that otherwise will not bond with one another anticipates the story "Of a Mirror and a Bell," in *Kwaidan*, about a woman who regrets her gift of the metal mirror to be used for the casting of a temple bell. Hearn sought in Japan what had pleased him in the West: stories about ghostly and tantalizing experience beyond his cultural inheritance and to some extent beyond his own unprompted imagining.

We can get a sense of the importance of Hearn's ghosts by thinking of Maxine Hong Kingston's *The Woman Warrior*, which she subtitles "Memoirs of a Girlhood among Ghosts." In recreating her own, or rather her family's, wandering past, Kingston focuses on those individuals who, in the old China, are shunned by family or community, who become voiceless, ostracized, unconnected. Without family they are also without a means of telling their story, and it is as ghosts, coming back to tell their stories, that they find some meaning. A tight and closed society creates its ghosts by exclusion; it must listen to them as a form of punishment or reintegration, which, of course, is the role of the storyteller haunted herself by the untold tales and living, as Hearn puts it, as a "civilized nomad." Kingston's look backward at her exiled and suffering aunt—among her other ghosts—finds in a rigid society a family and community mythology as rich as it was cruel.[21]

It is this richness in the untold and the unclassified that appeals to Hearn. Although his own past lay elsewhere, its ghosts maybe less available, he encountered in Japanese stories a satisfactory substitute. The emphasis on ghost stories indicates his conviction that Old Japan redeemed itself in the fullness of its imagination, in the creation of stories about those individuals banned from the society or punished by its inflexibility. Hence the ghost stories complement his usually less probing, less searching comments about pre-Meiji Japan, so that Hearn's New Japan (not unlike Kingston's or Hearn's America) emerges as at once full of energy, powerful, and admirable, while unredeemably vacuous.

3   Professor Chamberlain says that no one could
     understand Lafcadio Hearn who did not take into
     account his belief in ghosts.
                              —Elizabeth Bisland, *Life and Letters*
                                          of Lafcadio Hearn

A large proportion of Japanese ghosts are the spirits of women, those deserted in love or badly treated by family, who return for vengeance or unfinished business or to give warnings to the living. Ghosts often depicted, in the popular woodblocks of the ukiyo-e and in Kabuki, widely familiar figures who won posthumous identity in a society not known for attending to the needs of individuals. For in narratives of pain and suffering it is the personal crisis, the individual's history, that comes to matter. The ghost of the disfigured woman Oiwa, for example, returned in various terrifying ways to her callous and finally murderous husband, her vengeance a typical and extremely popular topic in the art and theater of late Edo and Meiji times. Hearn tells many stories about such forlorn and tormented ghosts, their examples offering vaguely moral lessons, however bizarre, to readers. And he finds moral complexity behind the Japanese stories about suffering women, appreciating in the tales strains of social criticism reminiscent of his muckraking journalism.

Readers of Japanese folk stories differ in the kinds of moral interpretations they choose to make. Some see the stories, relative to Western counterparts, as basically amoral; some see the Edo emphasis on stories about women as clear reflections of and pointed lessons about a civilization in transition.[22] Hearn is as torn on this matter as on most. Just as he emphasizes the moral power of Shakespeare while arguing that no good book was ever written for a moral purpose (see chapter 5), so he thinks of the Japanese stories in contradictory ways. Besides the implied comparison between a civilization that is complex, if also repressive enough to have ghosts, and a civilization too dedicated to power and money to evoke cultural depth, Hearn may share some of the contemporary Japanese dissatisfaction with the social inequities and ostracism suffered in historic Japan. But it also makes sense to think of Hearn aligning himself with the spirits of that earlier era; ever more exiled in contemporary Japan, he found his home with those sections of the community, those ghosts of the past, excluded like himself from the new order.

In a late essay in *Kwaidan*, written at a time when he is perhaps anticipating his early death, Hearn has this to say: "I should like, when my time comes, to be laid away in some Buddhist graveyard [as indeed he was] of the ancient kind,—so that my ghostly company should be ancient, caring nothing for the fashions and the changes and the disintegrations of Meiji."[23] Finally, in Hearn's moral pantheon ancient Japan, regardless of its failings, always outshone the modern, and the strongest signs of the ancient civilization lay in the ghostly, whose company Hearn kept in his writings as well as in his imagined place of burial.

Hearn's emphasis on the plight of women, on their dignity and power, speaks to his complicated attitudes about the relations of the sexes. Marcel Robert, in his biography of Hearn, says that in Japan "women no longer frightened him."[24] This is partly true perhaps; it seems more likely that Hearn insulated himself from the kind of women who had frightened him and chose someone he could keep in a certain role. He even insisted to his wife that he would prefer that she not learn English—and this in spite of his own struggles with Japanese. Hearn's responses to women are so ambivalent that there seems no reconciling opposite positions, as, for example, that women are goddesses, if they resemble his mother (or that advanced civilizations believe in a female god) or that women are inferior, if only because of relative physical "weaknesses." He commonly associates women with a greater power for evil than men; they are, he says, far more likely to be wicked.[25] Throughout his writings worship of one type of woman emerges as the converse of his fear of another.

There is a further ambivalence, as Robert points out, on the issue of race. Hearn's descriptions of black women in Cincinnati and Martinique, for example, suggest a powerful attraction based primarily on race, and, whether Setsu reflected a continuation of this pattern or a move beyond it, Hearn always seemed to associate sexual power with racial difference. Indirectly at least, the Fuji essay testifies to his lasting fear of women, and the ghost stories themselves make clear Hearn's fascination with the power of women over men, even from beyond the grave, which indebtedness to borrowed folklore or the currency of the tales will not entirely account for. Punished or punishing women, however much they are Hearn's personal inventions, play a major role in his Japanese tales.

Introducing the "weird tales" of *Kwaidan*, Hearn speaks of his discovery of the story of Yuki Onna, the Snow Woman: "One queer tale, 'Yuki-Onna,' was told me by a farmer of Chofu, Nishitama-gori, in Musachi province, as a legend of his native village. Whether it has ever been written in Japanese I do not know; but the extraordinary belief which it records used certainly to exist in most parts of Japan, and in many curious forms."[26] The comments are interesting. "Yuki Onna" was one of the best known of Japanese legends, popular in various arts and an established story in Japanese history, as Hearn must have been aware, since he himself had written about the legend in letters and in *Glimpses of Unfamiliar Japan*.[27] Possibly he means here only the specific account of the Snow Woman. In any case, Hearn says that he made his discovery in a characteristic way, from an ordinary Japanese person, as if he were collecting folklore. And he does precisely that when he searches for his material—while using a ploy common among fiction writers to authenticate their storytelling.[28]

Hearn's gathering of tales often began in conversation with his wife or a guide, or it developed out of his reading of an old collection. Sometimes he asked his wife to present her version of a traditional tale; sometimes he posed a problem to a translator, a person not necessarily gifted in English, who would (for pay) give him a literal translation of stories about a particular topic. Hearn could be quite acerbic about these materials, dismissing them out of hand or insisting on new versions. His published stories were not "translations" in the way his renderings of Loti or Gautier or Maupassant had been. They were, instead, his revised equivalents of the stories, which remained for him linguistically unavailable, as the French stories did not, although there is in both a love of the exotic, of the "queer" and "extraordinary" nature of events touching on everyday life.

The exoticism of the stories, in Earl R. Miner's distinction, was at once cultural and chronological.[29] Besides being known everywhere in Japan, they also had for the most part long histories. Hearn's introductions to the *kwaidan* emphasize both features:

More than seven hundred years ago, at Dan-no-ura, in the Straits of Shimonoséki, was fought the last battle of the long contest between the Heiké, or Taira clan, and the Genji, or Minamoto clan. ("The Story of Mimi-Nashi-Hoichi")

A long time ago, in the town of Niigata, in the province of Echizen, there lived a man called Nagao Chosei. ("The Story of O-Tei")

In the era of Bummei [1469–86] there was a young samurai called Tomotada in the service of Hatakéyama Yoshimuné, the Lord of Noto. ("The Story of Aoyagi")[30]

For the story of "Yuki Onna" Hearn opens in a slightly different way:

In a village of Musashi Province, there lived two woodcutters: Mosaku and Minokichi. At the time of which I am speaking, Mosaku was an old man; and Minokichi, his apprentice, was a lad of eighteen years. Every day they went together to a forest situated about five miles from their village. On the way to that forest there is a wide river to cross; and there is a ferry-boat.[31]

Instead of a particular historical time, he offers the vague "time of which I am speaking." That time becomes, after a few sentences, an indeterminate present instead of a vaguely distant past; except for the province itself, Hearn gives only the names and the ages of the woodcutters. He uses the same understated tone to begin the story— without the powerful adjectives he so often employs—and the story, like the other ghostly or weird accounts in *Kwaidan*, can hardly be anticipated by the matter-of-fact beginning. Hearn, who has difficulty with Kipling's matter-of-factness, almost always introduces his ghost stories with a kind of understatement. He begins with politeness or respect for the material, entering with deference into the world of his stories and gaining personal authority without appropriation. He still, so to speak, transforms his form, appropriating the stories *as* stories, so that they become Hearn's *kwaidan* rather than just other translations from the Japanese.

Yuki Onna, the Snow Woman, visits the two woodcutters when they sleep, trapped by a snowstorm on the wrong side of a river. After killing the old man, the Snow Woman is struck by Minokichi's handsome appearance and spares his life. Later, as a pretty young woman, she meets Minokichi and seduces him into marriage. In her undisguised state she had told him that, if he is allowed to live, he must keep the secret of their meeting for the rest of his life, but, alas, loving his wife and wanting to confide in her, he tells her after many years about his interlude with the beautiful Snow Woman. Instantly, she reveals herself to be Yuki Onna, reviles him for his folly, and threatens to kill him if he is ever unkind to their children. She then disappears.

A story such as "Yuki-Onna" supposes a supernatural threshold, a kind of synapse between a common— sometimes a very common—person and an uncommon stranger from another realm. At times humorous, as when the priest in "Common Sense" creates a bodhisattva from a badger, the encounters in Hearn's Japanese stories usually focus on overwhelming love, as in "The Story of Chugoro," wherein a young military retainer is ravished by the daughter of a god, who (as if to reverse the Western fairy tale) turns at last into a frog. The play with illusion and love, reminiscent of John Keats's *Lamia* and "La Belle Dame sans Merci," or stories from Gautier (*One of Cleopatra's Nights*) that Hearn translated, runs throughout the Japanese books. Usually, the supernatural visitor is a woman, a beautiful young woman, who seduces or falls in love with a young man. Even a story such as "Kimiko" (in the collection *Kokoro*), which seems an inversion of the usual practice, plays with the same elements. Kimiko, trained as a geisha to please men, is loved by and finally loves in return a handsome and wealthy young man. Instead of a Cinderella ending, with the marriage of the two unlikely lovers, the story allows Kimiko to write her own extended script. Renouncing her pleasure, she runs off to a nunnery, from which she returns only briefly, unseen by her former lover, to visit the man's child. Self-discipline, generous love, respect for social order: These take precedence over the passion and destruction described in other stories. More common is the sequence of "Urashima," in which love perishes from a failure of illusion, and the beautiful goddess, or ghost, *and* her fisherman lover lose what has become everything in their lives.

How close these stories were to Hearn's own concerns can be seen in his autobiographical fragments, including those published first by Elizabeth Bisland in *Life and Letters* and others scattered throughout the various books. I have mentioned the evocation of Hearn's mother in *Out of the East*, in which the writer, overwhelmed, almost seems to stop to remember a presence: a storyteller's beautiful voice, a world of sunshine and laughter, the gratification of someone caring entirely and generously for him alone. Is this any less a fairy tale than those he borrows from Japanese folklore? Could Hearn write about any topic without mediating personal experience into extremes of comfort and pain? In *Kwaidan* Hearn introduces two personal sketches, along with three of his continuing studies of insects, their habits and legends, which bring some of his preoccupations together.

"Horai," which translates to "Fairyland," is a brief allegory based on the Japanese myth that Horai, an almost perfect country of pleasure and reward, existed for the Japanese, much like the Muslim afterlife or some golden age or pastoral landscape in Greek or Renaissance literature. Horai in this revery becomes Japan itself, a country so natively beautiful, so perfect in its civil virtues, that it has needed no alternative utopia. As in most nostalgic visions, however, it is loss that dominates, and Hearn focuses on the changes making Horai into a Western, a masculine, country, in which the magic and the laughter have gone. In words he uses elsewhere, the Japanese "have been unlearning" in recent history,[32] losing the necessary selflessness of ideal civilization and replacing it with the rapacious self of Western models.

Hearn's autobiographical account in *Kwaidan*, "Hi-Mawari" ("The Sunflower"), looks back to boyhood summers spent in Wales:

On the wooded hill behind the house Robert and I are looking for fairy-rings. Robert is eight years old, comely, and very wise;—I am a little more than seven,—and I reverence Robert. It is a glowing August day; and the warm air is filled with sharp sweet scents of resin. "

The story is nostalgic, as its opening suggests, and it is about another kind of encounter than with fairies, although the experience turns out to be comparable in effect. Like the story in *Kokoro* about a blind and unprepossessing woman, whose voice beggars description, "Hi-Miwari" tells of the enchanting, overwhelming power of music. A harper affects him no less than the street singer, except that here the sound returns in memory after forty-five years. Hearn and Robert speak about goblins and their habitats until they recognize that the harper has come to the house: "But what a harper! Not like the hoary minstrels of the picture-books. A swarthy, sturdy, unkempt vagabond, with black bold eyes under scowling black brows." The meeting begins with disappointment and irritation, because the harper sings a song that the boy has heard sung by his mother. Soon the man's voice changes into "witchcraft," at once ineffably beautiful and terribly eerie: "Instinctively I fear that man;—I almost hate him; and I feel myself flushing with anger and shame because of his power to move me thus."[33]

When the harper has gone, taking without acknowledgment the boys' sixpence, Hearn and his friend wonder whether they have heard a goblin or a fairy, then settle for a Gypsy, which "is nearly as bad," since Gypsies "steal children." Gypsies steal children, and goblins steal souls. "Hi-Mawari" expresses in its few pages Hearn's powerful combining of the supernatural and the psychological, the personal and the collective. His own recollection feeds on the same interests and fear that inspirit his more formal ghost stories, pointing to the force of his lifelong ghosts, the voices of loss and separation.

Like "Ululation," the story of the harper rests on an understanding of silence, which is a recurrent and powerful element in much of Hearn's writing—witness the silence on Mount Fuji, the silence of Urashima's underwater kingdom, the ineffable silence of the interior of shrines and temples, the unbearable silence preceding most of the supernatural episodes in his stories. Before the various priests he describes face their macabre trials of will and belief, they undergo a trial of silence—so does the samurai who takes on the burden of intense weight requested by the goddess of childbearing. Hearn's translation from a story of Pierre Loti epitomizes his own preoccupation with the profundities of silence in connection with his understanding of Japan: "I have the impression," he says, "of penetrating suddenly into the silence of an incomprehensible past."[34] Silence in Hearn's stories provides the psychological space between the howling of the dog or the beating of the pestle, but also between the social and the

private, the lived and the remembered. "Ghosts," as Edith
Wharton wrote, introducing her book of that title, "to
make themselves manifest, require two conditions abhor-
rent to the modern mind: silence and continuity."[35]
Hearn, in a more personal way, said much the same. In "A
Ghost" he writes about "the knowledge that a strange silence is ever deepening about one's life, and . . . in that
silence there are ghosts."[36] In that silence, too, is the stuff
of art, which is never far in Lafcadio Hearn from the world
of ghosts.

The story of "Hi-Mawari," in form a revery, concludes
with three observations: Hearn mentions having seen
"only yesterday" a sunflower, which has prompted his
memory; he remembers Robert and himself "on that
Welsh hill," while wondering about Robert's "sea-change"
into adulthood; and he ends with the odd quotation:
"Greater love hath no man than this, that a man lay down
his life for his friend." Odd, because he has not spoken of
real friends, only of fleeting memories and a lost playmate,
with the hint once again of lost parents. Memory of the
harper, himself a wanderer, has brought the writer-
wanderer back to thoughts of loss and distance, time and
separation. Robert, on the other hand, is a kind of double,
an acquaintance long unknown and now, if not dead, grown
into a middle-aged man, a visiting ghost, or "Presence," in
Hearn's mind, no less than the harper himself.[37] In his
lectures, Hearn writes appreciatively about doubles in literature, and he admired contemporaries such as Robert
Louis Stevenson who used them so effectively. Robert, the
harper, and the hinted whisper of the boys' mother all serve
as reminders that for Hearn the supernatural enters often,
if painfully, into the world he describes.

This and Hearn's other autobiographical fragments—
about being locked in the dark room in Sarah Brenane's
house—illustrate how close Hearn's writing so often
comes to the experience of the uncanny.[38] There is always
something implied in the silences, something beyond the
described person or event, something concealed in the

folding of history and the unfolding of narrative. For Sigmund Freud (in his famous 1919 essay on "The Uncanny"), "an uncanny experience occurs either when infantile complexes which have been repressed are once more revived by some impression, or when primitive beliefs which have been surmounted seem once more to be confirmed."[39] This could stand as a specific analysis of Hearn's writing, which explores personal "impression," reaches back to forgotten memory (his own or a collective memory), and (not *or*) touches directly the relation between personal tension and "primitive beliefs."

The uncanny—*unheimlich* in German—also captures the homeless quality that Hearn, the "civilized nomad," never forgets. *Heimlich* suggests both *home* and *secret*, among its various synonyms, and these speak directly to Hearn's writing situation. His ghost stories play with ideas of uprooted, lost people who discover secret and frightening truths, about themselves, to some extent, and about a discomforting world. The story of Robert and the harper explores the same material in a more overtly personal way.

What I am suggesting is the intimacy in Hearn's writing between reveries on the one hand and ghost or other kinds of stories on the other. Hearn's "gestalt" conviction that bits and fragments of writing would somehow come together regardless of their subject and despite his lack of planning makes good sense. If never entirely whole books, these writings come together, in a sense, as one book: diverse in its topics, combining sociology with folklore, narrative with essay, diatribe with contemplation. The Japanese writings are all parts of a long exploration of that meeting place between two worlds, East and West, to be sure, but also the mundane and uncanny; they take place at a point where something unknown, troubling, and never fully stated confronts the writer with the ghosts of his past. This is perhaps why Hearn is so much more than a travel writer or guide to Japan. Japan is only one creation of a restless mind—a mind, in Wordsworth's famous line, "for ever Voyaging through strange seas of Thought, alone."[40]

[5]
Western Critic in an Eastern World

1   Although I believe Tolstoi is perfectly right, I could
not lecture to you—I could not fulfil my duties in this
university—by strictly observing his principles. Were I
to do that, I should be obliged to tell you that
hundreds of books famous in English literature are
essentially bad books, and that you ought not to read
them at all; whereas I am engaged for the purpose of
pointing out to you the literary merits of those very
books.

        —Lafcadio Hearn, from a lecture
at Tokyo Imperial University

Few statements could be odder or carry more irony than
this to Hearn's undergraduate students at the Tokyo Imperial University (later Tokyo University). Having lectured
for several years on British and American literature, Hearn
now tells the students that his teaching is fundamentally
unreliable, for, while he has insisted through the course of
lectures on the high value of British and American authors,
he comes around to warning students of his own disin-
genuousness. Much of what he has praised he has been
obliged to praise, a matter of professional expediency.
Western literatures are full of authors undeserving of attention, and he has been guilty of misrepresentation. Lis-
tener beware!

The radical simplicity of Tolstoi's "What is Art" fascinated Hearn while evidently forcing him to awkward ac-

knowledgment of cross purposes. As he tells his students, "art" for Tolstoi is a creation of the bourgeoisie and before them of the aristocracy, groups too removed from life to understand what genuine art should address because they lust after artifice instead of truth. Tolstoi urges art without artifice, the process itself defined by the potential audience of unspoiled, more fully human readers and viewers. Peasants and other working people, still able to think clearly and knowing truth from falsehood, set an unspoken higher standard by rejecting what generally passes for art.

Tolstoi's reverse elitism, his early version of Russian "socialist realism," implied (where Tolstoi was not explicit) a rejection of his own previous works and an impossible, not to say ill-conceived, ideal of art. Hearn objects elsewhere to similarly encompassing theories, and he admits to disagreement with specific aspects of Tolstoi's arguments, when, for example, he defends Kipling against Tolstoi as a writer of the people. At the same time, his long insistence on the importance of common people, his intent before coming to Japan to speak for and through ordinary lives, indicates how close he could come to sharing, if not appropriating, the ideas in "What is Art?" He felt, too, that literary study could benefit from Tolstoi's admonitions: "A time must come when the scholar will not be ashamed to write in the language of the common people."[1]

The problem lies in the antithetical nature of Hearn's views. "The worst books," he says elsewhere, "are better than the average reader," and (with perhaps ambiguous application) "there seems to be for vulgar people a very great attraction to the unintelligible." Ignoring dozens of his own comments about the "usually dull public," peasants presumably among them—as about the specialized nature of art or the need for literary critics to clarify literary matters—Hearn imposes overly simple assumptions about morality and social class on what in other writings he acknowledges to be a complex, if not unfathomable, topic.[2] As if this were not enough, he fails to question in

Tolstoi what he no doubt recognized as a tacit repudiation of his own kind of work. Delighted to use the thesaurus, trained to find the precise "needle-point of truth,"[3] Hearn is a writer whom Tolstoi would have dismissed out of hand. This does not stop him from telling students that Tolstoi is more right than wrong, that his principles undercut Hearn's own, that they are, fundamentally, impossible to counter.

The appeal to Tolstoi illustrates Hearn's contradictory ideas not only about himself and his job but equally about his adopted country and its literature—along with the discomfort he must have felt as a professor of English in a Japanese university.[4] Paradoxically, as I shall suggest, his praise of Tolstoi reflects an underlying generosity toward his students and an insight into their needs that undercut many of his pronouncements about the canons and qualities of Western literature.

2   The difference between the great critic and the
     common person is chiefly that the great critic knows
     how to read, and that the common person does not.
     —Lafcadio Hearn, *Talks to Writers*

Hearn, who had gone as a journalist to Japan, practiced journalism for only a few months in Kobe, where he adopted an altogether different voice and wrote for a different Western audience than his unseen readers in Boston, say, or London, or Berlin, who were the consumers of his primary essays and books about Japan. Kobe proved an exceptional interlude in Hearn's Japanese life, because the journalist, almost from the beginning, had become a teacher, and teaching provided his main source of income, giving him a standard of living and a level of financial security he had never before enjoyed while making possible his residence in the beautiful samurai house in Matsue and the large house he lived in during the final years in Tokyo. If only for economic reasons, teaching served to distinguish his life in Japan from earlier phases, when financial security for any length of time had been an elusive dream.

Hearn taught at four Japanese institutions: the schools in Matsue and Kumamoto and two universities in Tokyo. (In Matsue he taught in both the middle school and the normal school.) How eager he was for any of the assignments is hard to say. He accepted the Matsue job after turning down a less lucrative offer by another school, and he said he went to Kumamoto because the pay was higher and the climate suited him better. His justifications make sense, though perhaps no more so than the previous reasons he had offered for choosing New Orleans, Martinique, and the other stages of his long journey.

About the post at Tokyo Imperial University Hearn expressed relatively little enthusiasm. Instead of accepting the offer as a gesture well meant and graciously tendered, he remained suspicious about the treatment he received, negotiating with care and finally accepting after doubting that he would. Nor did he make any great efforts to keep the jobs he found. His first report to the university authorities told them that the system was a mess, his efforts wasted, and the students badly treated: "The undersigned does not feel satisfied with the results of his work during the past academic year. . . . Even an instructor of much Superior attainments and Experience would scarcely have succeeded better."[5] During and after being caught in a bureaucratic tussle having to do with his citizenship and salary, he had nothing but criticism for the institution and the governmental power structure it represented. This, despite the fact that the university paid him at the same rate as foreign nationals and made every effort to honor his talents. Some of his ex-colleagues who spoke about Hearn at a commemorative meeting in Kobe in 1940 expressed lasting irritation with his version of the facts.[6] They were probably justified. Hearn construed information in his own slanted fashion, finding malice or obstruction where it was not intended—and sometimes offering bizarre interpretations of what he saw. Once he was certain that a visiting American woman, curious about his lectures, had come as a spy to undermine his standing. She was, after all, dressed ominously in black.

With the exception of the schools in Matsue, Hearn invariably found ways to discredit the institutions for which he worked. Granting that institutions of higher learning are no more exempt from folly and red tape than businesses or newspapers, it was, and is, true that they tend to leave people free time for their own writing. Tokyo Imperial University and, for the last months of his life, Waseda University provided generous incomes and almost unlimited privacy to Hearn, who shunned colleagues and public events, indeed almost any responsibility beyond the classroom. For a brief time he enjoyed the company of a few foreign teachers, best of whom, to his surprise, was a Jesuit priest, but none of these relationships—they were hardly friendships—continued for long. Worrying about proper dress or decorum and manifestly uncomfortable in his public roles, he served, unlike Chamberlain or Fenollosa, more as a writer-in-residence than as a full-time member of the faculty. Despite his isolation, however, he established himself as a gifted, if idiosyncratic, teacher, caring about the students themselves and immersed in the topics he discussed.

The poet Edward Thomas, in his early study of Hearn, insisted that Hearn "was not a born schoolmaster."[7] Probably the opposite is nearer to the truth. Whether writing private letters or addressing the larger audience implicit in his books, Hearn seems to have imagined himself in the role of teacher. His introduction to the novel *Chita: A Memory of Last Isle*, written when he lived in New Orleans, describes the bayous of Louisiana and traditions of the region as if the author were primarily intent on informing his reader about topography and history. The same is true for his writings about the West Indies, his descriptions of Creole cooking, and, in the early days in Cincinnati, his muckraking articles, when he unmasked tricksters, provided information about racial tensions, and delivered to his readers the sordid underlife of the city.

It is just as true of the Japanese books, wherein Lafcadio Hearn speaks as the Western representative to foreign parts, intent on providing a vital picture of the world he sees and convincing his audience that what he describes has great value, value that he, above all, has been privileged to recognize. For the many American and European readers of his essays and his books, Hearn wrote with full awareness of their curiosity and limited knowledge; like a good teacher, he used his personal experience to address their needs. Tacitly in these writings Hearn acknowledged his own former ignorance, interpreting for a public who may have known little less than he himself had known before setting off for the East. Sometimes Hearn's enthusiasm allows him a patronizing aside; sometimes he recognizes that his audience may reject his point of view. Usually he writes with patience and generosity about the world he has discovered and wants to share.

Similar qualities emerged in his classroom teaching. One student, speaking at the 1940 Kobe conference, recollected "the passion with which he treated his subject, . . . as if poetry was his life."[8] Another recalled that he taught his students painstakingly and in clear English, describing fondly the "plain-looking," dedicated person who, in an unprepossessing yet determined way, changed his life.[9] Hearn actually supported one student financially through a course of study at the university. More than forty years later, students remembered him vividly, remarking on his dress, his voice, which according to one student resembled "a golden bell," and his uncharacteristic hospitality to a select few.[10] Students who had known Hearn in Matsue and Kumamoto and later studied with him in the university agreed that, setting aside his brilliance in the lecture hall, he was a changed man: less social, far less giving of his time, impatient to be back at his own writing desk.

Whether he wanted to compensate for his privacy or

whether the privacy afforded him untroubled time for study and reflection, Hearn spent long hours preparing lectures on British and American poets, dramatists, and essayists. If we accept that his writings are those of someone who chose publication as his larger classroom, then his classroom lectures offer texts that are at once alternative and complementary to his professional writing. There is, of course, one large difference. Hearn intended none of the lectures to be published, and, because he lectured from brief notes, he left no finished manuscripts behind. "They are only dictated lectures," he wrote, "dictated out of my head. . . . Were I to rewrite each of them ten or fifteen times, I might print them. But that would not be worth while [*sic*]."[11] Since time and again Hearn insisted on careful proofreading, on a "text" sufficiently polished to serve as a final draft, materials still inchoate or at an early stage of thinking would not have been acceptable to him for publication. His attendance to such matters indicates that Hearn, though disparaging himself as a writer of whole books, always prided himself on being a stylist. He was irritated by the publication of other writers' unfinished works and would have been appalled, no doubt, had he known that his lectures would be published after his death.[12] In a variety of collections they were published, transcribed by Hearn's students, who had been told (during the lectures) when to insert a comma or how to spell a word, almost as if—Hearn's protests notwithstanding—he was dictating to an amanuensis with eventual publication in mind.[13]

The course of lectures lasted over six years, from September 1896 until March 1903. This means that during the time Hearn wrote some of his most probing analyses of Eastern religions and Japanese culture, he was defining for himself and his students the literature of another world, a world he questionably claimed as his own, that of Chaucer and Shakespeare, Pope and Robert Browning, Blake and Swinburne. His assignments at the universities called for

massive surveys of English literature along with lectures
based on topics of his own choosing, including commen-
taries on nature poetry, recent trends in British and American literature, and Western literary indebtedness to Greek
and Roman writers.

The reader will find here [wrote John Erskine in 1922] a close
record of Hearn's daily instruction to his Japanese class in English
literature. The record is unique. I never read these chapters without marvelling at their simplicity, at the volume . . . of Hearn's
critical faculty, and at the integrity of his character. The simplicity of the lectures is deceptive. . . . Simple as each lecture
seems, the mass effect of them all, delivered day in and day out,
on all the great themes of Western literature, is nothing short of
titanic.[14]

A quarter century after they were given, Erskine found in
Hearn's lectures the highest critical thinking paired with
the finest exposition. Erskine saw this work as modern,
"mature," indeed, as "criticism of the first order."[15] Not
all readers of the lectures have agreed with his assessment.
George Gould, a biased critic at best, called the lectures
embarrassingly incompetent, and appropriately so, given
that they were the work of an uneducated writer. Edmund
Gosse (whose own historical studies Hearn attended to)
thought them beautifully presented, if finally derivative.[16]
The fullest and best assessment of Hearn's lectures
comes from Beongcheon Yu, whose rich and sympathetic
study of Hearn also presents the best-informed estimate of
his various writings. Yu argues that Hearn furthered
Goethe's long-ignored plea for a world literature, that he
called on his students to appreciate international trends
and the relation of their own writers to foreign models.[17]
Hearn in this view built the bridge between East and West
begun by his Japanese books, though from a reverse perspective. In Erskine's words, with which Yu tacitly agrees:
"Others as well as he have explained Japan to the West, but
who else has explained the West to Japan?"[18] The question,
as the Tolstoi passage suggests, is far more complicated
than its implied answer, for Hearn's explanations are nei-

ther straightforward nor altogether clear in their purposes. Nor do they point inevitably to a new world literature.

More than he acknowledged, the lectures offered Hearn an opportunity for sorting out his larger views on literature as well as identifying—if only implicitly—the nature of his own writing as a part of the tradition he explored. Hearn knew where some of his deficiencies lay and made no excuses, even when he wrote to his American friend Ellwood Hendrick, for example, about a possible lecture series in the United States:

The main result of holding a chair of English literature for six years has been to convince me that I know very little about English literature, and never could learn very much. I have learned enough, indeed, to lecture upon the general history of English literature, without the use of notes or books; and I have been able to lecture upon the leading poets and prose-writers of the later periods. But I have not the scholarship needed for the development and exercise of the critical faculty, in the proper sense of the term. I know nothing of Anglo-Saxon: and my knowledge of the relation of English literature to other European literature is limited to the later French and English romantic and realistic periods. Under these circumstances you might well ask how I could fill my chair. The fact is that I never made any false pretences, and never applied for the post. I realised my deficiencies; but I soon felt where I might become strong, and I taught literature as the expression of emotion and sentiment,—as the representation of life. In considering a poet I tried to explain the quality and the powers of the emotion that he produces. In short, I based my teaching altogether upon appeals to the imagination and the emotions of my pupils,—and they have been satisfied (though the fact may signify little, because their imagination is so unlike our own).[19]

Sometimes Hearn's diffidence seems to be an appeal to his correspondents to contradict him, to tell him how able he is and how much he underplays his own powers. Possibly Hearn made such an appeal to Hendrick; he had spoken similarly to Chamberlain—including the times when he berated Chamberlain for not rescuing him from Kumamoto or not securing for him a job in Tokyo. If, as he says, he did not actively seek the Tokyo position, he made unmistakably clear to his friends that he deserved a teaching post in the capital. The old pattern in Hearn's letters of speaking aggressively about his needs and then, when criticized or reprimanded, falling back on his lack of opportunity and intellectual capacity, meant that he went his critic one better, almost boasting about his awareness of his own failures. After all, he says, "I never made any false pretences."

Modesty is always a slippery thing to define, and when it enters our comments on profession it becomes particularly slippery. Probably Hearn did think that he knew "very little," though his comment about lecturing without notes or books sounds a little like self-promotion. Did he actually believe conventional wisdom that knowledge of Anglo-Saxon was crucial to full understanding of the field? In almost any other context he would have challenged such an idea as mere academic shibboleth. By this time he was fully aware of what worked and what did not work, what was essential and what was fatuous, in the course of study for which he was responsible. Recognition of professional limitations did not stop him from pursuing good scholarship or possessing a "critical faculty, in the proper sense of the term."

The assignments clearly posed difficulties for Hearn, who preferred his own yokes and fretted under those of others, whether imposed by newspaper editors, publishers, or officials in a university. Apart from the necessity of honoring a relatively fixed curriculum, he worked at further disadvantages. To a great extent he was himself learning what he taught to students, understandably so, given that this exiled and largely self-taught man had acquired neither formal academic training nor the wealth that allows for leisurely reading. Unlike Fenollosa, who arrived in Japan fresh from his Harvard education and more or less familiar with the materials he would teach, Hearn had read widely but randomly; to his teaching he brought only the advantage of eager curiosity and a retentive mind.

Breadth of knowledge was at most a brief problem. Hearn not only amassed an astonishing wealth of information, digesting his reading in a way that made his lectures lucid and authoritative, he also ranged easily and gracefully over the field. It is surprising how much reading of Western literature he managed in these years and, in addition to belles lettres, how much scientific and social scientific literature he continued to find useful. The man who was writing elegant studies of Japanese inner life or religious belief was also, consistently and habitually, reorienting himself in the West.

Writing at a time when the "profession of English literature" floundered in its inauspicious infancy, when Oxford and Cambridge universities were moving slowly and reluctantly to an acceptance of nonphilological approaches to an English curriculum, Hearn offered a rich and informative history of British literature. Certainly his two-volume *Interpretations of Literature* (1926) compares favorably with George Saintsbury's *English Literature of the Nineteenth Century,* for example, and with the many other literary histories, including Andrew Lang's *History of English Literature* and Reuben P. Halleck's *History of English Literature,* which appeared in those years. For all his Japanese jingoism, it is hard to imagine Hearn competing in folly with Walter Raleigh, who, a few years later, was to match in fancy a hundred English professors against a hundred "Bosch" professors as a means to speed the war effort.[20] (Hearn had made unfair equations between Japanese and Chinese soldiers during the Sino-Japanese War.) He is, recognizably, a man with fin-de-siècle sympathies, for whom art is self-evidently of fundamental importance. At the same time, he appreciates crucial relationships of art to society and argues for aesthetic development as for moral imperatives in a way that would not have appealed to purist contemporary aesthetes like the symbolist Arthur Symons.

Hearn lectured on such a variety of literary figures and topics that summary or overview would be difficult. To give some sense of his thinking and his range, we might glance at his comments on four very different writers, two British, two Americans: Shakespeare and George Borrow, Edgar Allan Poe and Walt Whitman.

"I must try to tell you in the shortest possible way," Hearn said to his students, "how Shakespeare is great, why he is great, and what are those particular qualities of mind by which he surpasses all other men." His comment makes several matters obvious. First, as I have mentioned before, Hearn thinks of criticism as "a psychological study," the pursuit of the man through the writings.[21] Second, and in spite of countless disclaimers about not wanting to judge, he does want to judge, to rank authors for his students. Shakespeare is a "genius," and Hearn's hierarchy of major and minor writers, those with genius and those with talent, characterizes his entire vision of Western literature. But why is Shakespeare in a class by himself? Because, he says, Shakespeare is the most profoundly moral writer and the least consciously moral. "The relationship of morals to literature is very intimate"; it is also complex. "Life does not mean one morality," Hearn writes, and "no great work was ever written for a moral purpose." Paradoxically, morality remains a central issue for him, however loosely defined, as if he cannot finally approve of a writer who is not a teacher of moral principles. "I told you long ago," he tells his students, "that no bad man ever could write good poetry."[22] If this kind of smugness is relatively rare in the lectures, preoccupation with the topic of morality and literature is not. "In a certain sense," he says,

every great poet is a great priest. . . . Now there are two ways in which the great poet figures as a priest. One is by simply reflecting and teaching the best moral thought of his own country and time. The other . . . is by teaching men to think in entirely new ways about whole-truth.[23]

Besides his moral powers, Shakespeare is a great artist because he has the vision and language of a poet and because he reaches "whole-truth," or some synthetic vision, more completely than other writers. Many of Hearn's positions, and some of his contradictory attitudes, are drawn from Herbert Spencer, who wrote an influential study called *Education* and whose range of interests extended into the arts or, in Hearn's view, necessitated certain interpretations of the arts. "In short, the position of Spencer that moral beauty is far superior to intellectual beauty, ought to be a satisfactory guide. . . . If moral beauty be the very highest form of beauty, then the highest possible form of art should be that which expresses it." This leads him to a position beyond Spencer's and far more reflective of his own erotic perspectives: "I should say that the highest form of art must necessarily be such art as produces upon the beholder the same moral effect that the passion of love produces in a generous lover."[24]

Hearn's judgments about literary morality may be as traditional as they are derivative. His understanding of collective or racial memory is another matter. When he thinks of Shakespeare and memory, he enters a new order of literary complexity, anticipating at the same time twentieth-century notions of "the death of the author" or the subordination of author to text. As with Roland Barthes or Michel Foucault, such arguments can cut two ways. What distinguishes Shakespeare from a lesser writer is his "large sympathy" and intuition, which Hearn identifies with "a kind of inherited memory." "Uneducated" and therefore unspoiled as a writer, Shakespeare also possesses the past of other people. He is John Keats's idea of the chameleon poet but almost preternaturally large, the holder of secrets, the teller of endless tales: "The self is now seen not to be one but many."[25] More than a priest, he seems to Hearn a kind of incorporative being, a limitless text. Genius that he is, he triumphs as a collective voice, in a sense less a person than a creative force.

Hearn appreciates Shakespeare for his collective powers in a more parochial sense. Emphasizing, like Andrew Lang and so many other literary historians of the day, a tight bond between race and literature, he thinks of Shakespeare as a reliable Anglo-Saxon, implying throughout the lectures that Anglo-Saxon virtues help explain the literary strengths of the English people. Paradoxically, then, Hearn holds up to his Japanese students a kind of racial ideal, embodied in Shakespeare and inimitable for other ethnic groups, Japanese included.

At another extreme from Shakespeare are "the strange . . . figures of the Eighteenth and Nineteenth Centuries," writers including William Blake, William Beckford, and Thomas Love Peacock. Particularly intriguing to Hearn is the eccentric novelist George Borrow, whose ancestry, Hearn thinks, is not European but, as a Gypsy, Oriental. Facts here are less important to him than associations:

> None of [Borrow's] books are, in the strict sense of the word, either novels or romances [he has said the same about Peacock]: they are all romantic narrative of things really felt and seen. He did not attempt any complete framework of story; there is no beginning and no end; there is no order; there is no sequence. I do not know how to define his method better than by telling you that most of his works resemble printed notebooks. Nevertheless, these books have a charm and a quality absolutely original. . . . [Borrow] perceived that the most ordinary incident of every day life could be made interesting.[26]

In such discussions it is clear that Hearn assesses his own methods and offers tacit justification for what he himself, as master of the odd, both attempts and achieves. Borrow, the outsider who wrote about outsiders (not to mention Borrow the man, with his terrible problems of sexuality and isolation), serves as a benchmark for Hearn himself, who can tell his students about the aberrant and the odd as a way of suggesting why and how he himself writes. Hearn also tests writers like "Monk" Lewis, whose terror and horrors now "merely disgust": "Skulls and bones and blood and lustful monsters do not frighten anybody to-day."[27] In other contexts, of course, they continue to frighten and to intrigue Lafcadio Hearn, whose lasting preoccupations with the psychology and effects of horror apparently seemed to him of another order, something less self-indulgent than Lewis's. Self-discipline, closely tied to literary form, is a virtue he has come to seek in others.

This raises once more the case of Edgar Allan Poe. Master of horror and someone as appealing to Hearn as to the French writers whom he passionately extolled, Poe was his favorite American author. Poe stood out as "a brilliant, eccentric genius, . . . an uncomprehended enigma among men," as Hearn had already written in New Orleans.[28] The same hyperbole occurs in his Japanese lectures, where the anomaly of Poe's stature suggests Hearn's entire perspective on American literature, which, with the exception of a few writers, he tends to dismiss: "American literature really exists in very small quantities." That is primarily because "poetry is the test," and "America has produced very little poetry above the third class."[29] In fact, Poe is the single canonized author from the years before 1850 whom Hearn introduces to his students, and he speaks of Poe almost exclusively as a writer of stories.

Hearn had long appreciated Poe, perhaps even modeled himself on him. Calling himself "the Raven" as a young man, he was obviously reading Poe with pleasure and respect—and seeing affinities with his own ambitions. If Poe embodied storytelling of an order Hearn could not attain, he also served as a literary double, a fellow explorer of shadows and a believer in "composite ghosts." In a sense Poe defines for Hearn the aspirations of his own art, which seeks an unexpected power from things too dreadful to confront, tempering the fear by exquisiteness of form. Hearn writes: "A little of the element of fear enters into every great and noble emotion, and especially into the higher forms of aesthetic feeling. The sublime is more than the beautiful, because it is the beautiful capable of inspiring awe as well as admiration."[30]

All of Hearn's favorite notions come into play when he speaks of Poe. The short story "Shadow" allows "millions of dead . . . to form one shadow and to utter one voice."

What is true of Shakespeare, then, is true of a teller of tales like Poe. Beyond this, Poe achieves his composite identity through dreams, or rather nightmares, through his preoccupation with "the fear of dreams" and the "power of the horrible."[31] This vocabulary, informing the lectures, informs no less the stories and books about Japan, which Hearn in part sees through eyes trained by a reading of Poe. He may well be, as he has been called, a kind of "Orientalized Poe,"[32] though he is a writer of vignettes and a cultural translator rather than a writer of carefully articulated stories.

Unlike Poe, whose stories to Hearn were formal triumphs, Walt Whitman "had no form." The very phrasing suggests Hearn's baffled, perhaps even unexamined, response to Whitman, whose writings overlap his own almost as fully as those of Poe. Sounding much like the early Henry James, Hearn could call Whitman "the voice of a giant beneath the volcano," a writer "earthy and of the earth." This does not redeem him as an artist, since the volcano prompts a negative image, the "lava flow of lust."[33] Whitman is indecent as well as imaginatively stunted: "Perhaps the only original part in [Whitman's work] . . . is the part treating of the sexual relations as divine and wonderful and worthy of all reverence." Then again, he says, "this part is not suitable for consideration in the class room;—neither is it altogether worthy of commendation."[34] Interestingly, Hearn can turn around and attack Whitman's critics for calling him "immoral." That, he says, is not the issue—even as he makes it the issue. Interestingly, too, he commends Blake for identical bravery, and he tells his students repeatedly that issues of love, physical love included, define the differences between Eastern and Western literatures and are central to considerations of most Western authors.

More than this, Hearn's repeated pleas to his students about the importance of "romantic rebellion," the need to continue the poetic revolution of the early part of the century and to apply its principles to Japanese creativity, make it difficult to understand his disgust with Whitman's work. Form, as he says elsewhere, is essential to poetry, if we accept that form needs constantly to be reformed, adapted to new circumstances in a process of evolution that includes literature as well as society. Whitman may simply be too radical for him to accept, and all the more so if "no changes of any importance [in literature] can be made suddenly and with good results. . . . All progress must be gradual." Following Spencer, who once again trips him into contradictions, Hearn insists that literary evolution must be slow and is often retrograde: "All literature progresses by undulations—by a series of actions and reactions—not by a steady flow."[35] This perception opposes his other positions about the importance of literary revolutions, for which the "Romantic Revolution" serves as model. Although a writer such as Whitman is—if anyone is—a romantic revolutionary, Hearn turns around his inventiveness, demanding less "eccentricity" and more tradition.

If Hearn never came to the "pact" that Ezra Pound realized out of his struggle with Whitman, that may have been because Whitman had qualities too close for Hearn's comfort. Another exile in his own land, another writer fascinated by the East (the mother of languages, the place of origin for both men), another idiosyncratic and impractical writer, Whitman loomed as a dangerous influence as well as a rival.

But why did Hearn fail to see in Whitman the man of the people, of common men and women, he who celebrated "the anonymous acts of ordinary life?"[36] Part of the problem may have been politics. Hearn grew to distrust democracy in both the United States and Japan (where he preferred the military party), and he scorned "the Whitmanesque ideal of democracy. That ideal was the heart-felt expression of a free state that has gone by."[37] It is also possible that he recognized and resented another cultural mediator: the spokesman for American life performing as he himself performed in translating Japanese culture for the West. Whitman, as Emerson's "American poet," answers a large call, transforming self and rejecting his past in the process, appropriating the country he represented, transcending his ugly roots at the same time. Whereas Hearn hides himself and some of his topics behind enigmatic Japanese words or unstated longings, Whitman sings loudly out of himself (or his personae), celebrating love and sex, serving as the genial giver, the provider of things. Hearn's own, quiet, self-subduing presentation is no less ambitious; it is merely less grandiose. And these are not so much questions of style or form as of the positioning of self in a culture of one's own making. How far one could push parallels about mother figures, or generic views of women, I am not sure, but it is clear that there is far more in common between Whitman and Hearn than Hearn himself could admit—except between the lines of his troubled assessments.

Hearn had difficulty being generous about contemporary writers, saying many times (in and out of his lectures) that with few exceptions modern British and American literature lay in the doldrums, guided by inadequate philosophy and waiting for new models. "The last quarter of the century is almost silent, so far as the higher literature is concerned."[38] (He often exempts Henry James, as the best American writer, and Kipling, as the best British writer.) Possibly Whitman seemed, despite *his* affinities for Spencer's positions, unphilosophic as well as undisciplined. In any case, the giants of literature are dead for Hearn, and mediocrity is the order of the day. The same is true, he implies, of Japanese literature, which needs a comparable overhaul on Western principles. The problem is that Hearn advocates change at one time and finds it impossible at another, and this is a basic, almost crippling weakness in his bridge between East and West.

Using a parenthesis and a collective pronoun, Hearn says in his letter to Hendrick that his Japanese students probably can't understand what he is teaching, "because their imagination is so unlike our own." The comment epitomizes Hearn's insistent claims for a fundamental and problematic gulf—racial and cultural—between Westerners and Japanese. Although he wavers in his attitudes just as he wavers on his commitment to Japan and the Japanese, his conviction of difference and otherness seems absolute: "It is impossible for any who have never lived here . . . to understand the enormous difference between the thought and feeling of the Japanese and our own."[39] The longer he stayed in Japan, the more convinced he became of insuperable barriers to communication. "The Japanese do not understand Western thought at all," he says;[40] no more can Westerners understand the Japanese.

Given such a premise, it is remarkable how much Hearn managed to assist his students, finding ways to deal with their misunderstandings or their lack of knowledge. In little as well as large ways he showed them how to make parallels between their own and Western literatures. He often comments on Japanese topics, neatly adjusting his remarks to the audience (whose needs he addresses directly), while speaking in the competing voices of two disparate worlds. He refers to the Old English "wanderer" as a kind of "ronin" (a retainer without a lord), to the *Anglo-Saxon Chronicle* being like the Japanese *Nihongi*, to Urashima resembling a Japanese Rip Van Winkle; he talks of the potential use of Sir Walter Scott's poems for Japanese writers, of the need for good translation. Matthew Arnold appears (improbably but amusingly) as "the son of the old-fashioned samurai, educated strictly according to the ancient system, and then suddenly introduced to the new condition of *Meiji*."[41] Hearn makes historical as well as literary references, drawing parallels when possible—in the service of the impossible. That is, he speaks with the conviction of absurdity, of his own limitations, in a situation that should have provided him with an ideal opportunity and in fact convinced him of the folly of an English literary curriculum for his students. Not only "do the Japanese not understand Western thought at all, at least on its emotional side," but "the foreign teacher is trusted only as an intellectual machine."[42]

Throughout the lectures Hearn sounds less like a man of

letters than an academic, whose knowledge seems different in kind from that of the writer of the Japanese books. The Western professor might be discussing the literary merits of, say, William Blake and in a lecture on mysticism scarcely allude to the Eastern mysticism he explored concurrently in *Gleanings in Buddha-Fields* or *Exotics and Retrospectives*. The question arises, To what extent did he see poets like Blake or traditions like "the Romantic tradition" (with which he claims allegiance) from the perspective of his Japanese experiences? To what extent did he redefine as well as define it? Did he bring new insights to accepted masterpieces? Did he question accepted canons? My concern here is with the implicit gulf in Hearn's understanding between the Western books he introduced to students and the Japanese world in which he immersed himself for the books he published.

When he discovered little-known Japanese folk stories, Hearn delighted in making them his own. Feelings mattered to him more than judgments. He will not say, for example, that a particular poem is a work of genius or the best in the language, although he will honor (as he does with English equivalents) those works that have withstood the test of time. In speaking of British literature throughout his lectures, Hearn insists on the importance of emotional response—making the literary work one's own—but he seems intent on giving his students less a sense of the experience of literature than an idea of its standing. "Remember this," he might say, as if with an exam or public reckoning in mind, or "You must not forget these facts," or please note this book's "actual rank."[43]

Hearn's approach to Western literature bears on his entire approach to the Japanese and his confidence in his students. Hence, while he promises a new phase of Japanese literature that will have learned from the West and tells his students what they must do to bring about change—if Japan is not to lag behind the rest of the world—several of his students recalled with mixed feelings that he also dissuaded them from pursuing literary careers, ostensibly because Japan needed socially useful people rather than authors at this stage in its history. According to one student, "He discouraged his boys from taking up literature as their life work. . . . He contended that our country needed men who were familiar with practical sciences."[44] Since Hearn elsewhere and repeatedly bemoans the new, practical Japan, the advice has to be seen either as his tacit dismissal of modern Japanese literature (which he rarely mentions) or as helpful advice to young men who might waste their talents or live with a sense of failure in the country Hearn saw emerging. Beyond this lay Hearn's insecure feelings about his own career and about the sufferings he had found necessary in its pursuit. Who would want one's students to suffer or starve? Still, the ambivalent feelings as to the worth and the future of Japanese authorship remain inadequately addressed, let alone resolved.

More is at stake here than the economic prospects for Japanese authors. For the lectures on British literature imply, with peculiar variants, an acceptance of that literature as normative and superior. No one, Hearn says, can match Shakespeare, and, while this may well be true, Hearn insists on its being absolutely, unarguably true. English writers as a whole are Shakespeare writ large. George Borrow and the other eccentric "gypsies" offer intriguing byways without altering the larger judgments and the assumed canons. To put this bluntly, Hearn's distinct, even idiosyncratic, views do not involve a serious reexamination of the literature that, in some cases, he now reads for the first time *as* his heritage.

An important indication of Hearn's sense of conflict occurs in a letter he writes to his old friend, Henry Watkin: "When one has lived alone five years in a Buddhist atmosphere," he says, "one naturally becomes penetrated by the thoughts that hover in it; my whole thinking, in spite of my long studies of Spencer and of Schopenhauer [has been changed]. I do not mean that I am a Buddhist, but I mean that the inherited ancestral feelings about the universe—the Occidental ideas every Englishman has—

have been totally transformed."[45] What he says bears directly on the Japanese books, less so on the unpublished lectures to students, where his thinking seems at most partly transformed.

It would be unfair to expect of Hearn either an entirely new approach to British and American literature or a radical assimilation of East and West in lectures designed for another purpose. It is not unfair to expect him to have applied more of his appreciation of traditional Japanese literature to the Western authors he discussed—or to have questioned directly some of the parochial or nationalistic Westerners he drew from when preparing his lectures. The point is that his enthusiasm for Japanese literature remains surprisingly disconnected from his approaches to literature of the Western world. Whereas he could dismiss "realistic" Western painting of his era as crude and unnatural, pointing to Hokusai or other painters of the ukiyo-e tradition as true artists, he made clear to his students that Western literature set standards unmatched by the Japanese, who were not likely to change the relative value of their literature in coming generations. To speak in such terms was to ascribe cultural no less than literary inferiority to Japan, a notion that in much of his published writing Hearn rejected with contempt.

3   To be a European in the Orient *always* involves being
        a consciousness set apart from, and unequal to, its
        surroundings.
                                        —Edward Said, *Orientalism*

If for most Westerners, Japan remained the country of china dolls, miniature beauty, pretty but finally meaningless values, Hearn stood firmly as an advocate and apologist on the other side. He insisted on the dignity of the Japanese, which explains a part of his insistence on their political and military potential, their future force in the world. He recounted stories of suffering in modern as well as ancient Japan. He approached Japanese life with the kind of sympathy he praised in the best of Western writers. Why then has he so little to say about contemporary Japanese poets and novelists? Why does he show more respect for the writers of Western society, a society he has implicitly rejected as a place to live or as his temperamental home?

One way of addressing such questions is to think about recent approaches to cross-cultural issues. A particularly important concern has to do with "mainstream" British and American literature used as comparison with what is likely to be a relatively unknown literature from another culture. The perceived importance of literature (however *that* word should be defined) often reflects its national genesis: English and American literatures tend to be more valued than those of, say, Australia or the Caribbean, even when the books are written in English. (Ireland, with its ties to Britain and the United States, offers an intriguing exception.) A further complication obviously comes from translation, which can put literature in yet another ghetto. Not too many books from the "Third World" become commercial or critical successes (or objects of academic study) in Britain and the United States. Part of the problem is contextual: Again, readers do not know such books in their historical or broadly cultural circumstances; if they read at all, they can more comfortably assess or even understand books of their own country in relation to an established canon.

However much Hearn honored Japan as an industrializing nation—indeed, the first non-Western country to industrialize—and however much he would have bridled at the modern term *Third World*, his attraction to Japan had much to do with its otherness, its distance, its difference, even its vulnerability. Perhaps novels and any other modern or derivative literature represented yet another threat to the Japan that he had chosen to love, so that his choice of books took him inevitably backward in history— to folklore, legend, mythology. It would seem likely that Hearn contrasted the development of Western literature with the static and relatively unchanging nature of Japanese works. Often writing about Japanese poetic forms, Hearn loves the restrictions of these syllabic works and the historical continuity of their genres,[46] but this does not mean, when he comes to assess them for students, that he can find them rivals to Western books in power or authority. In other words, Hearn's own love of paradox points to a basic paradox in his own thinking—and perhaps in the thinking of almost anyone who seeks to learn about, let alone to reside in, another culture. When he taught Japanese students about his native literature (assuming that to be either British or American), he reverted to his role as outsider, alien. Ernest Fenollosa's rejection of Hearn's union of Herbert Spencer and Buddhism suggests what Hearn himself effected in his lectures and essays. Now he did not strive for a unified vision, the very quality he sought and associated with home in the early days, and he hardly shows commitment to a "world literature." West apparently reverted to West, East to East.

Hearn's twin intellectual worlds, that of his public writing and that of the university, suggest how he lived and thought during the final years in Japan. When someone like Percival Lowell had finished with Japan, writing his books to sum up his impressions, he realized what he could learn, what was impenetrable and what was exportable in the world he had explored. Lowell wrote *Occult Japan* and took up his second career, building an observatory, addressing himself to questions about Mars and the other planets, no doubt aware that the new field of discovery offered an extension of the Japanese experience at a more intense and, for Lowell, more satisfying level. Hearn never achieved that insight. After the enthusiasm of his early years had dwindled, or came only sporadically, he continued to seek what had vanished from his life, equating his creativity with the emotional responses of his early years as if, having lost the one world, he did not know where he might turn next.

John Erskine was right to say that Hearn's strength as a

critic lay in "throwing a clear light on genuine literary experience—on the emotions which the books under discussion actually give us."[47] For this was the underlying strength of his writings about Japan. Chamberlain knew more; Fenollosa had a finer sense of Japanese arts; Edward Morse was better informed about architecture and handicrafts; Percival Lowell arrived at clearer opinions about religion and culture. It remained for Hearn to explore, in a sense, from within, to ask probing questions about his own emotional response, so that he could translate his feelings for his audience. And this was precisely what he accomplished for his students, to whom he spoke personally, warmly, engagedly. He showed his students why he cared and how they, too, might care. At the same time, as his letter to Ellwood Hendrick makes clear, Hearn recognized and insisted on an unbridgeable gulf between himself and his listeners. It is possible that Hearn came to differentiate his imagination from that of Westerners as well as from that of Japanese students, seeing himself emotionally (as well as physically) separate from the world around, or from the world in which he wrote.

Let me return briefly to Hearn's defense of Tolstoi when he summarized his lectures toward the close of his career at Tokyo Imperial University. In that lecture he confesses that a significant part of English literature is of little value and that he himself has been forced into hierarchical judgments or an excessive inclusiveness at odds with his students' needs. These remarks compete with both private and public comments, whether about imaginative visions or about the future of Japanese literature or the relative importance of a British literary canon.

In the Tolstoi discussion Hearn quietly suggests to students a revolutionary point of view. They, the students, are evidently the "common" readers; they are the ones who must set the standards of art in a new Japan. Hearn urges them to question him and the educational system he must perforce represent. He has said throughout the lectures that Western literature is of no use to the Japanese when simply borrowed. It must serve as a stimulus, a temporary model, not as an institution to be imitated. Hearn's appeal to his students to keep reading, to make themselves the independent judges of what they encounter, may in a sense be hopeless, because the students read so poorly and because their responsibilities are not primarily directed toward the study or writing of literature. The hopelessness is comparable, however, to that which he himself feels about understanding Japan and its civilization—or life itself. Hearn is not an optimist. He offers students only small hope of sorting out the issues he deals with, inasmuch as he himself remains puzzled, dismayed, tugged in different directions. At the same time, he is freeing his students and, tacitly, elevating the Japanese art that, throughout the lectures, he has subordinated to norms of Western literature. He appeals to an understanding larger than his own, to possibilities he himself has not been able or allowed to fulfill.

[6]
Hearn and Japanese Civilization

1   Civilization is a cold and vapid humbug.
           —Lafcadio Hearn to Rudolph Matas

        The same waves wash the moles of the new-built
        California towns, but yesterday planted by the
        recentest race of men, and lave the faded but still
        gorgeous skirts of Asiatic lands, older than Abraham;
        while all between float milky-ways of coral isles, and
        low-lying, endless, unknown Archipelagoes and
        impenetrable Japans.
           —Herman Melville, *Moby-Dick*

In an era intrigued by concepts of civilization, Japan raised puzzling questions. If this was not a country civilized as Western countries were thought to be civilized, defined by the "progress" associated with industrial and military power, how did one come to terms with its continuity, its ancient *civility*, its qualities that would have to be included in any definition of civilized society? The very discussion was circular because, of course, the terms were overlapping and ill defined, but the questions persisted.[1] Before the reopening of Japan to the West, the archipelago remained "an unknown lump on our earth, and an undefined line on our charts."[2] Unfamiliarity did not stop writers who had never seen Japan from defining its characteristics or from doubting that an isolated and closed society could compare in any crucial ways with the civilized West. After Commodore Perry's breach of the "impenetrable" country, the issues became more complex, in part because of Western ambitions in Japan and Japanese national pride, in part because visitors to Japan imposed their own definitions on the changing society.

The matter of Japan's civilization remained a moot question in the developing field of anthropology because anthropologists more or less ignored Japan in favor of "primitive" societies, whether the Eskimos on Baffin Island or Maori in New Zealand.[3] Japan received tacit "civilized" status in being left to the scholars and tourists, many of whom associated it with lost civilizations of the West (again, Greece sometimes managed to be both East and West) and discovered in the Far East their own nostalgia.

Hearn was right to say that neither Japanese nor Westerners had provided an adequate cultural history of the country, and, while his own encounters with folklore and tradition suggest the methods of some contemporary anthropologists or at times draw information from men like Edward Tylor (*Primitive Culture*), the anthropologists themselves were elsewhere. Ruth Benedict's *Chrysanthemum and the Sword*, written after World War II, may have been the first extensive anthropological study of Japan, and even that had an inauspicious genesis.[4] Benedict had not been to the country she wrote about; her shrewd and insightful book is in essence a pastiche of other people's work, however subtly pulled together.

Although Westerners never claimed Japan to be a primitive country, either before or after its opening to the West, this did not make Japan's status as a civilization simple to those interested in the classification. Nor did the common comparison with weaker, more amorphous, or more exploited countries such as China and India necessarily confer—from a Western perspective—the independent power and accredited stature of a fully civilized nation. Lafcadio Hearn thought that Japan was in peril of becoming "an Anglo-Saxon province" on the one hand or being defeated militarily on the other. By citing China as an object lesson, Hearn pointed out to citizens of his adopted

MR. LAFCADIO HEARN

This sympathetic cartoon suggests the widespread view of Hearn as the transplanted international who had become Japanese. Illustration by John Henderson Garnsey, *The Critic* (10 April 1897).

country how close they were to economic exploitation, if not actual colonization. He argued that great diplomatic skill and subtle maneuvering, as well as military might would be necessary for Japan to survive with its own culture intact. When, in an essay on "The Genius of Japanese Civilization" (in *Kokoro*), Hearn begins with observations on military prowess, he seems to warn England and the United States about Japan's increasing power, before reminding the Japanese themselves that force of arms had protected their culture through the ages.

But how did East and West define that culture? Probably for most Western commentators, Japan was worthy of respect on the one hand and typically Oriental—or inconsequential—on the other. As for the Japanese, in early Meiji years they had moved aggressively to destroy Oriental affiliations and sought international recognition by wholesale Westernization. Felice Beato's photographs from that era show Japanese in improbable top hats and other parodic costumes of the West; they had not yet become protective about their own cultural history or fully recognized what Hearn insisted to be necessary: aggressive economic and political practices complemented by an isolationist social policy.

The top hats and ill-fitting Western suits marked an intermediate stage of crude Westernization, the antithesis of pre-Meiji separateness. Pertinent is Basil Hall Chamberlain's remark about the Japanese disappointment with Sir Edwin Arnold, when he lavished praise on a quaint or fantastic Japan and failed to mention the hundreds of miles of new railroad tracks or the growth of industrial might or the radical shifts in educational policy. At a time when Ernest Fenollosa and Edward Morse almost reeducated the Japanese themselves about their invaluable cultural heritage, the government of the country apparently cared little about indigenous art.[5] People who would later become national treasures (as artisans may in Japan) found themselves without work or respect. Yet within a few years, Fenollosa himself had outlived his evident usefulness in a country that had turned away from Western culture—from proposed plans to make English the national language, for example, or from blind imitation of Western painting.

Japan's great changes and obvious shifts in policy reflect and influence Western attitudes in the latter half of the nineteenth century.[6] To say that Japan received different treatment from the West than other so-called Oriental countries is probably true; it does not mean that Japan was always or automatically safe from Western domination or that its independent course came without great cost. *Impenetrable*, the word Melville applied to Japan—or "Japans"—at mid-century, suggests some of the anomalies in Western attitudes toward what was at first an unknown and later an enigmatic land. The word *impenetrable* reflects a common equation for European and American travelers between the country and its women—witness some of Pierre Loti's crude and self-indulgent views. Japan as an ancient land and as a beautiful, remote woman stayed in the minds of Western travelers throughout the nineteenth century and appealed, as I have suggested, to Hearn himself, who neither altogether escaped the perspectives of fellow Westerners nor sorted out his personal ambivalences.

Writers contemporary with Melville sometimes admitted that their attraction to the country began with thoughts about its women, who were acknowledged to be exquisitely graceful, tantalizingly withdrawn, surprisingly untouched by false modesty, and at the same time refined to an astonishing degree.[7] Sir Edwin Arnold, writing poems about "The Musume" ("girl" or "daughter," with the suggestion of "mistress"), essentially defined Japan by its women, whom he found, predictably, handsomer than Japanese men and more civilized. Women devoted to pleasure or committed to serve raised no questions about Japan's future, its commercial and military developments, or the ways in which, for Arnold, it was racing dangerously after Western manners and institutions. His *Japonica*, a tribute to Japan at the conclusion of his year's residence in

1892, spoke only incidentally of history, politics, and social conditions during a long revery about the writer in a charmed but threatened land.[8]

Fenollosa's thinking was more sophisticated and much more informed than Arnold's, yet Fenollosa also conceived of Eastern civilization as "feminine," Western as "masculine" (except in certain paradoxical ways by which Western love symbolized the feminine and Eastern "martial faith" the masculine). In his Phi Beta Kappa poem of 1892 Fenollosa prophesied a "two-fold marriage" between cultural virtues of the contrasting cultures, his metaphor suggesting the aims of his own encounter with Japan.[9] Admiring Japanese art and committed, like his friend Sturgis Bigelow, to Buddhism, Fenollosa still managed to anticipate Western repositories for Japanese art and to conceive of a higher civilization predicated on the best qualities of East and West. "Fuji at Sunrise" extended the masculine-feminine metaphor, with the mountain a beautiful woman joined in sexual love by the rising "prince of day."[10] Fenollosa's opposition of East and West provided a common enough way of assessing Japan in relation to the West. Percival Lowell defined East-West differences as a function of the masculine West dominating a feminine East, which accounted for the aggressive "imagination" of the West and the subtle, unimaginative "taste" of the East. Stretching the metaphor further, Lowell found similarity between Japan and France, popularly the most effeminate as well as feminine nation in Europe.

Possibly borrowing from Lowell, Hearn himself imagined Japan as another France, or, rather, as a potential France for the Orient. He does not make clear why a civilization having so many virtues should have to aspire to become like the French, but this relative placing of Japan suggests the underlying ambivalences of his thinking. In fact, Hearn's competing statements about Japan make clear his own tendency to see Japan in terms of a feminine metaphor, as if the country were his lover and he its chronically disheartened suitor. Japan for Hearn can be a torturing spirit, a holder of secrets, a source of torment; it can also be a teasing mistress, a comforting mother, or a gentle woman, a land whose very gods, he says, contrast with the patriarchal and punishing Judeo-Christian god of the West.[11] If, on the other hand, Hearn argues at times for the innate superiority of men, this did not stop him from idolizing women such as Elizabeth Bisland or from thinking about his wife as a simple but elevated creature. Regardless of contradictions, Hearn's views of Japanese civilization included a central place for women, whom he respects for all the reasons Edwin Arnold praises and for others as well. In his "Woman's Diary" he speaks with profound feeling for an ordinary, suffering woman, resident of Tokyo in the new Japan.[12] He often tells stories about solitary or abandoned or mistreated or heroic women, past and present, who ultimately embody for him the essence of Japanese civility.

In more tentative or provisional ways than Fenollosa, Hearn could imagine a marriage of East and West, although "brief affair" might better describe what he recommended to the Japanese. Indeed, his language—at rare moments—suggests something closer to rape. Attempting to come to terms with "progressive" implications of Western technology, he can say: "The Oriental, with his power of retaining health under conditions under which no European could live, with his savage daring when roused, with his inborn cunning, lacks only the superior knowledge of civilization to be the equal of the European in warfare as well as in industry."[13]

In this unusually absolute passage, Hearn condemns both East and West, the one for its backward state and "savage" temperament, the other for its military bias, its industrial and practical civilization. Given such an equation, it is hard to see how one might learn from the other. Civilization was, he thought, a state to be realized as well as a term to be redefined, and for Japanese living in a time of enormous change, civilization amounted to the merits of past excellence *wedded* to present Western power. Temperamentally appalled by Spencerian notions of progress for Japan, Hearn nevertheless tried to square his usual faith in Japan's future with Spencer's sanguine assumptions. Spencer's evolutionary theories promised an improving future based on inherited characteristics rather than on the lottery of genetic chance and appealed to the self-made men of late nineteenth-century commerce and industry. Hearn himself at times subscribed to Andrew Carnegie's image of progress as the power of the express train, though it is worth remembering his silence about train journeys in most of his Japanese writings. In a sense he urged for Japan what he found intolerable in his own life. And no doubt it was hard to ignore entirely what the sociologist Max Weber described as the pervasive "rationalization" of modern life, the subordination of everything to material well-being or technological advancement, the world of nature not excluded.[14]

Unlike Fenollosa, who repudiated the idea, Hearn proposed another sort of marriage, an intellectual-spiritual union, that is, between Spencerian philosophy and Eastern religions, notably Japanese Buddhism. Here, too, Spencer raised awkward problems for Hearn. In assuming, for example, the kinship between economic and cultural hegemony—to use Antonio Gramsci's overused word—he never entirely comes to terms with Spencer's dismissal of less powerful races and un-Westernized cultures, even when the arguments touched him personally. Concluding *Japan: An Attempt at Interpretation*, Hearn quotes from and comments on letters written by his mentor to Japanese officials in Meiji Japan, among them recommendations that the government stamp out marriage between Japanese and foreigners.

To your remaining question respecting the intermarriage of foreigners and Japanese [Spencer writes], which you say is "now very much agitated among our scholars and politicians" and which you say is "one of the most difficult problems," my reply is that, as rationally answered, there is no difficulty at all. It should be positively forbidden.[15]

Hearn, who in more independent moods thinks of "all good races" being "mixed," ignores his master's prescription when praising Spencer's dogmatic and distant views, no doubt because marriage with a Japanese woman defined a great deal of his Japanese experience, providing material for his books and obviously shaping his life. In private letters Hearn seldom speaks about his future in Japan without mentioning his wife and the family dependent on him. Could he have endorsed Spencer's arrogant positions to such an extent that he would reject his own chosen way of life? Did he overlook this one recommendation for the sake of his greater argument: an appeal to the Japanese to maintain their traditional culture and their independence from the West? Or did Spencer's argument force reflections on his own marriage and on the conditions of his exile as imprisonment in Japan? Whatever the case, Hearn's struggling respect for Japan—for its women, its traditions, its political and military ambitions—offers a complex and fascinating key to Western attitudes at the turn of the century while opening at least a small window into the realities of historical Japan.

2   The murmuring mass of an unknown language
     constitutes a delicious protection, envelops the
     foreigner (provided the country is not hostile to him)
     in an auditory film which halts at his ears all the
     alienations of the mother tongue. . . . Hence, in
     foreign countries, what a respite! Here I am protected
     against stupidity, vulgarity, vanity, worldliness,
     nationality, normality.
                            —Roland Barthes, *The Empire of Signs*

Hearn's physical and social isolation in his later years reflected disillusionment with the lived reality of modern Japan; it did not affect his passionate commitment to Japan and Japanese civilization in the books and articles he wrote. Some of his articles are nostalgic returns, including one evocative essay about a summer stay in Izumo, which tells, like the "Yokohama" essay, of former illusions or hopes necessarily mitigated by time and experience. Because Izumo means so much to him, Hearn clings to it as a Japanese ideal, well aware that he made the Province of the Gods more than it could have been, more beautiful, more emotionally satisfying in his written memory, the *Glimpses of Unfamiliar Japan*. In a frank assessment of his own thoughts, he acknowledges that the relatively untouched or traditional qualities of the western region move him profoundly as a reminder of earlier times. He also makes clear that eastern Japan, the Japan of Tokyo and the Kansai—Osaka, Kobe, Kyoto—has entered into a disquieting future, to which with reluctance and misgivings he has committed the remainder of his life.[16]

Hearn needed no physical return for this sort of revery. Many of his later writings collected in *Romance of the Milky Way, and Other Studies and Stories* (1905) and elsewhere are fugitive pieces and are included as such without apology.[17] Stylistically as well as emotionally, he writes more or less the same kinds of books throughout his last decade. The later studies tend to reflect reading more than physical experience (especially when contrasted with *Glimpses*), albeit presenting Western readers with the same sorts of episode, idea, social custom, or literary evocation introduced in the other books. During the final years, however, Hearn ventured a different writing project, not altogether unrelated to the lectures on British and American literature or even to his articles (uncollected during his lifetime) from the Kobe *Chronicle*.[18]

Japan: An Attempt at Interpretation was in press when Hearn died in 1904. It is not only his most sustained work, as I have suggested, but it is also his most scholarly, or overtly scholarly: a synopsis of ideas spread through the other writings now drawn together into sustained argument. *Argument* may not be the right word for a text that announces, describes, narrates, but which insists repeatedly—and with ample illustration—on the religious foundations of Japanese culture. The book is "conservative" (Hearn's term borrowed from Spencer's letters to Japanese correspondents). It holds up the Old Japan as a model for the future, urges the retention of traditional values, and more or less prays for a Japan that will live through the war against Russia with vital powers and values intact.

Japan announces those values, or Hearn's interpretation of them, more categorically than any other of his books and is in this sense a summing-up. It reads, however, like a long meditation on the question of Japanese civilization. "The reader scarcely needs to be reminded," he says, "that a civilization less evolved than our own, and intellectually remote from us, is not on that account to be regarded as necessarily inferior in all respects. Hellenic civilization at its best represented an early stage of sociological evolution; yet the arts which it developed still furnish our supreme and unapproachable ideals of beauty." Hearn manifestly does need to remind his readers. He provides here an astonishing range of related information: mainly religious but also political, even military. When talking of the war with Russia, he alludes to earlier Japanese strategies, to historical developments and economic conditions, even to military hardware. Reflections on modern developments are, however, built on a deep awareness of historical origins, including class distinctions, domestic customs, and, above all, religious belief: "The history of Japan is really the history of her religion."[19]

This statement signals Hearn's fulfillment of his earlier, almost despairing comment that he would be forced to write a treatise on Buddhism, other avenues to understanding having closed. It sounds, too, like the comment he made about "the Odd," as if his dissatisfaction with his writing pushed him into illogical and arbitrary choices: I can't write fiction; therefore I shall write about the grotesque and the weird; I can't understand Japan sufficiently; therefore I shall write about Buddhism. *Japan* is in this sense a less ambitious, or at least more detached, book, for it stands at a clear remove from the sort of ordinary, lived

experience Hearn had predicted he would write about before arriving in Japan and that he managed so eloquently in
Glimpses. He writes *Japan* as if posthumously, looking
back on his past life in a more studied, if no less intro-
verted, manner, distancing himself from the essays that
had established his reputation.

Readers of *Japan* do not experience Hearn's exhausting
climb up the steps of temples or the slopes of Fuji; we do
not see the mists lying on Lake Shinji or hear the clogs
tripping across wooden bridges. We are out of the world of
Urashima and the stories glowing with legend and oral
traditions. Hearn reverts to some of his editorial rhetoric
for the papers in Cincinnati and New Orleans, yet even
when writing journalism he had often been the experienc-
ing witness for his reader, entering strange rooms, meeting
unexpected characters, discovering social anomalies, hearing undecipherable tongues. In another sense, there may
be more connection between Hearn's writing about barber
lore in Cincinnati or slave conditions in Martinique and
Glimpses than between *Glimpses* and *Japan.* For, while the
topic Japan binds these two books, the whole approach to
Japan seems to have changed. The sense of Arcadia has
confessedly gone: "Sooner or later, if you dwell long with
them [the Japanese], your contentment will prove to have
much in common with the happiness of dreams. You will
never forget the dream—never; but it will lift at last."[20]

To a certain extent, Hearn's sense of disillusion, the loss
of dreams, has to do with language, or with the unaccom-
modating nature of the Japanese language and its effect on
his understanding. Somehow liberated as well as fascinated by his first experiences in Japan, Hearn exulted in the
sounds he heard, his anxieties offset, perhaps, by that film
of innocence, the protection (as Roland Barthes says)
"against stupidity, vulgarity, vanity, worldliness, nationality, normality." The fact of a new language in a new
culture promised experience without responsibilities.

Naming is as important to him in *Glimpses* as the discoveries themselves, whether he speaks of "the gods with the long weird names" (and gives them in *romanji,* the Western spelling) or delights in teasing readers about their ignorance: "You do not know what an uguisu [a small song bird] is?" "Hai yako hanishino," he writes aptly in one notebook, "I have something to tell you."[21] A messenger from Japan, he thinks in the early years that he will master the language, just as he had mastered French, so that he will be speaking with the full privilege of the initiated. The desire continues after the awareness of his language failure becomes clear. When he speaks about the Buddhist tombs in the Kobudera graveyard, he delights in the names given to the dead, which are different from their previous names and which have the quality of something ethereal, "gnostic," in his sense of words as beings. By this time, however, the Japanese language has become an impediment to happiness, a sign of his isolation. "What liberates," as Hans Jonas writes in his study of Gnosticism, "is the knowledge of who we were, what we became; wherefrom we are redeemed."[22] Hearn's own essentially identical questions rest on his conviction of the power of words, which underlies his appreciation of other writers (Pater, Poe, Baudelaire, Kipling) and matters intensely for his sense of self. Now he comes to the realization of himself as an alien writing in a foreign language about linguistic signs he could perhaps intuit but not decipher.

In *Japan* Hearn speaks of the Japanese language less as a delightful puzzle than as an insurmountable barrier. It was, he wrote, "unspeakably difficult to learn."[23] Without actually saying that he has never learned Japanese, he argues here that no Westerner *can* learn the language, especially the written language, and for that reason alone must remain alien and unaccepted. Hearn ignores what must have been uncanny linguistic talent on the part of Percival Lowell, say, or Basil Hall Chamberlain, whose knowledge of Japanese was legendary, though he does single out one other (Japanese-born) Westerner whose fluency went well beyond his own. His comments touch basic truths, nevertheless, about the nature of exile and about the specific problems faced by those who encounter Japan.

There is a sense in which Hearn's remark about exclusion looks backward to centuries-old beliefs about Oriental languages. Walt Whitman's phrase "the house of maternity," implying the Orient as mother and mother of the West, had as a corollary the idea of the "mother tongue," the original language.[24] Hearn's own association of the East and motherhood was, then, both personal (in the sense of his conviction of return to his maternal heritage) and conventional, part of a shared creation—the Orient—which predates the Oriental movement of the nineteenth century, the recreation of the exotic East for Western purposes. His association of the notion of origins with the barriers of an impenetrable language seems to occur first in the later writings, which testify to a sense of failure along with exclusion.

No doubt the inability to learn Japanese had something to do with the decreasing amounts of naming in his later books, especially *Japan.* Instead of periodic and exploratory sentences punctuated by excited comma-dashes or strung together by semicolons (Hearn had an early reputation as "Old Semi-Colon"), he now writes more deliberately, more soberly, the syntax itself indicating the deflated self who writes. If this gives credence to Hearn's own assertions and assumes a connection between temperamental changes and literary style, still—for *Japan* at least—some accommodation has taken place. The following, for example, is a characteristic passage from *Glimpses of Unfamiliar Japan:*

Here are Hokusai's own figures walking about in straw raincoats, and immense mushroom-shaped hats of straw, and straw sandals,—bare-limbed peasants, deeply tanned by wind and sun; and patient-faced mothers with smiling bald babies on their backs, toddling by upon their geta (high, noisy, wooden clogs), and robed merchants squatting and smoking their little brass pipes among the countless riddles of their shops.

A contrasting passage from *Japan: An Attempt at Interpretation* almost shouts its differences:

Another development of ancestor-worship—the cult of gods presiding over crafts and callings—deserves special study. Unfortunately we are as yet little informed upon the subject. Anciently this worship must have been more definitely ordered and maintained than it is now. Occupations were hereditary; artisans were grouped into guilds—perhaps we might even say castes;—and each guild or caste then probably had its patron deity.[25]

Hearn speaks often of "sociology" in *Japan*, and he writes with a kind of detached authority (while invoking many other authorities) as he explores the signs and structure of the society rather than its ways of being, its phenomenological or experiential qualities. *Glimpses* obviously emphasizes impressions and sensations—everything from a quick glance at a mirror in a shrine to the smell of tatami mats or the colors of cloth for sale in the shops. Little of this enters *Japan*, the focus of which is meaning created through history and social patterns.

The titles of the books suggest further differences: *glimpses* indicating doors to be opened, a world to be explored; *attempt* indicating the difficulty of the whole enterprise, which is less that of "understanding" than of "interpretation." By the date of *Japan*, Hearn speaks of thousands of books about the country—most of them, he says, rubbish—and, while this echoes his early conviction that little new could be written about Japan, it is clear in *Glimpses* that he does feel able to offer a singular vision, his way of living and looking in the new land.

Shifts in perspective involve, to some extent, a subtle shift in values. While traditional Japan still appeals to Hearn, in *Japan* he speaks of it, quite simply, as lost: "Remember that here all is enchantment—that you have fallen under the spell of the dead—that all the lights and colors and the voices must fade away at last into emptiness and silence." He then draws his favorite parallel with Greek civilization, imagining a return to that "antique civilization" and pointing out that there, too, a modern visitor would fail to understand, for "no modern mind can really feel . . . as people used to feel some thirty centuries ago":

To witness the revival of some perished Greek civilization—to walk about the very Crotona of Pythagoras—to wander through the Syracuse of Theocritus—were not any more of a privilege than is the opportunity actually afforded us to study Japanese life. Indeed, from the evolutional point of view, it were less of a privilege—since Japan offers us the living spectacle of conditions older and psychologically much farther away from us, than those of any Greek period with which art and literature have made us closely acquainted.[26]

Here is the anthropological or historical vision, the counterpart of Hearn's early curiosity, which has been metamorphosed into patient and skeptical love.

An idyllic or utopian Japan that Hearn associates absolutely with the past and ambivalently with the new Japan presents only one side of his late interests, for these include the future as well as the historical culture. The chapter on "Jiujutsu" (from *Out of the East*) offers a good example. In this essay, written in 1897 with the Sino-Japanese War in mind, Hearn explores the military-psychological makeup that allowed the Japanese immediate success in international conflict. Defense as aggression is at the heart of his theory, which argues the inexorable, if still potential, power of a nation dedicated to self-discipline and large ideals.[27] Just as the new soldiers of Meiji Japan give their lives for the emperor (and Hearn sees this as praiseworthy), so the practitioners of jujitsu give themselves to the limited ends of their martial art. The tradition is that of the samurai: dedicated, sacrificing, wholly determined, whose powers are so automatic, so ingrained, that one individual can fight like a small army. (One of Hearn's consistent points is that, in contrast to the West, Japan could bear the costs of sacrifice: It was tougher and less selfish and would, through national policy and individual strengths, resist Western habits along with Western domination.)

Conscripted though they are under the 1873 law, the fighting men of the new army and navy inherit the virtues of their aristocratic forebears. Hearn is awed by their power, however troubled by the suffering and dislocation they may bring about. Indeed, he is almost jingoistic about Japanese treatment of the Chinese, just as he is later full of tribute for a country able to take on what he calls Europe's most powerful nation, the land of the Czars. He understands these struggles as part of a frightening and inevitable (and Spencerian) world force: "The aggressions of race upon race are fully in accord with the universal law of struggle—that perpetual struggle in which only the more capable survive. Inferior races must become subservient to higher races, or disappear before them."[28]

From the remoteness of his Tokyo room, Hearn delivers in *Japan* a final appeal to the country he loves (and hates) to use military and economic power for the preservation of a state that military and economic power would change forever.

How much Japan has changed "intrinsically," how much it has preserved its fundamental nature while adapting to Western modes of production and to vast increases in population, are questions still argued in Japan and the Western world. Commentators like Kurt Singer have suggested that the forms of Japan have changed, not the real Japan, which retains its traditional modes of thought and its assumptions about life.[29] Hence Hearn's own questions have remained key for later writers, no doubt because questions reflect hopes. Hearn prophesied a future based on his own longings, which meant his own definition of Japan, and, like Singer's, his hedge was that the Old Japan might not be apparent in the face of the New Japan. For him, ancestor worship of the Shinto faith and a sense of spiritual balance from Buddhism would always define the Japanese and the ways the Japanese have contended with the Western world. Spiritual purpose along with a certain Asian toughness (lack of imagination?) would allow Japan to prevail. Alas, he knew that it would not be the Japan he loved.

3   "You are there, because I was there." . . . Participant
           observation [in ethnography] obliges its practitioners
           to experience, at a bodily as well as intellectual level,
           the vicissitudes of translation. It requires arduous
           language learning, some degree of direct involvement
           and conversation, and often a derangement of personal
           and cultural expectations.
                    —James Clifford, "On Ethnographic Authority"

To put Hearn's mercurial and self-contradictory views in
perspective, we might remember anti-imperialist feelings
in Stephen Crane, William Dean Howells, and other Americans in the 1890s; or think of Joseph Conrad's excoriating
satire on the civilization of the Belgians in *Heart of Darkness*. In Conrad's nightmare story, brutal Europeans inflict
their greed and will to survive on people they consider
savages, lesser humans at best and subhumans if the truth
be known. Conrad, like Hearn, had read the monstrous
self-deluding, self-promoting tracts that justified the Con-
go as a personal fiefdom of Leopold II and the granting of
that prerogative by the combined European powers at the
Congress of Berlin in 1885. Conrad understood the activities of Kurtz in relation to half a century of racialist
thinking, its assumptions shared alike by French, English,
Germans, Belgians, Dutch. Civilization was that unexamined opposite of native savagery, whether the savages
were Australian, American, African, or Asian. For Conrad
the truly civilized were the best of the English; for Hearn
the truly civilized were those inhabitants of another
world, however much Western powers intruded into that
world.

From a distance of nearly a century, it may be easy to
fault both Hearn and Conrad for politically inadequate
views of imperialism and colonialism, as if writers could
extract themselves from the worlds in which they live or
were more exempt than others from personal inadequa-
cies. In fact, neither writer deserves condemnation. Like
Hearn, Conrad was an exile, probably too inclined to praise
English traditions, as Hearn was to praise Japanese. But

both explored with sympathy and astuteness worlds beyond their early imagining. Conrad, who mastered the language of his adopted country, was lucky enough to be able to write in the conventional genres of that country— however much, in his opinion, he improved them. Hearn neither adequately learned Japanese nor managed to write the novels and short stories expected in the West from a gifted writer. In this Hearn also differs from Robert Louis Stevenson, Kipling, and Henry James, all of whom used their exile for less risky literary purposes. But, of course, Hearn was typical of so many exiled writers of his generation who, whatever their success or chosen medium, struggled as he did with the issues of living and writing in a foreign land. Partly because he never resolved such issues in his life, remaining torn about Japan and doubtful about his career, Hearn has over the years been dismissed as merely fin de siècle. This is to underestimate the complexity of the age and of the person himself, the historical man who responded to a specific set of circumstances, not merely to a generic intellectual or cultural life at the turn of the century. I want to touch briefly in these final pages on a few of Hearn's Western legacies and what they may mean for his career and reputation.

In the late nineteenth-century America described by T. J. Jackson Lears, Hearn belonged to both the main culture and the counterculture, at once a progressivist and antiprogressivist, yearning for authentic experience, or, in his case, authentic experience *and* the writing that complements it.[30] Again his idolatry of Herbert Spencer placed him with the optimists, the dominant power groups who assumed the purposive, improving nature of a society organized for productivity and personal achievement, dedicated to efficiency and "rationalized" economic principles of living. Yet Hearn would have dismissed many aspects of this association, and with justice, since he saw little connection between a faith in material and cultural progress and easy optimism: "Civilization is a cold and vapid humbug." American civilization was something he criticized and tried to avoid, as his journeys to Martinique and Japan make clear.

Hearn's antiprogressive sentiments are more obviously evident and less ambivalent. "Anti-modernism," the widespread movement of disaffection with contemporary urban life, might serve as a general category for placing this solitary, disappointed man, who sailed in 1890 for Japan. Uninterested in ordinary personal comforts (however much attracted to sensuality), which he rejected as assiduously as his aunt, Sarah Brenane; committed to the importance of craftsmanship (like the arts and crafts advocates of his era); irritated by anything he considered to be over-civilized; recoiling from noisy and busy urban life and searching for some more satisfactory belief in the "self," Hearn typified many contemporaries who escaped into real or imagined exile. The Orient was a common haven for Westerners disillusioned with life at home and seeking more intense spiritual or physical experience in another culture. Like these contemporaries, Hearn arrived in Japan to discover a new self in an old civilization. Even his occasional militarism on Japan's behalf is a sign of his antimodernism—just as it would be for poets in the First World War and for Japanese writers like Yukio Mishima after the second.

Orientalism was as much a condition of European as of American thinking.[31] Hearn had read and enjoyed Gustave Flaubert and Gerard de Nerval as well as English and American Orientalists long before he arrived in Yokohama. He continued to read such authors after taking up residence in Japan. How much he was influenced by Orientalist assumptions, how much independence he gained with the experience of Japan, is hard to pin down. It is odd to think of him trying to follow Pierre Loti's tracks in Kyoto, even while speaking of Loti's idiosyncratic impressionism, his difference from Hearn himself.

Without question, Hearn's vision of Japan, and of Japan as a historical civilization, was highly selective. So aware of historical barbarities and social evils in the West, he remained oddly blind to comparable problems in Japan. Samurai standards of honor may have warranted attention; what of peasant revolts, a hallmark of the later Tokugawa era? The selective vision excluded such matters. Hearn might be described as someone, in Raymond Williams's thinking, who is aware of a "social totality" in which culture emerges or operates[32]—when, that is, he discusses England or America. Unlike his earlier assessments of societal ills and problems in Cincinnati, his writings about Japan are, in Friedrich Nietzsche's word, as "weightless" as his own existence, suspended between observation and hope, insight and longing. His assessment of Japan allows a separation, or divorce, by which the cultural qualities he seeks can be independent of the social world he reluctantly addresses. Possibly Hearn's response to Japan, as time went by, was to see it as overcivilized in a way comparable to the West he had left behind. This might explain some of the difficult confrontations and subdued writing in *Japan*. The more he knew, the less he was apt to approve, with the result that, consciously or unconsciously, he was forced to conjure a remembered idyll or accept an unattractive present. His reluctance to leave his study suggests how much he preferred the idyll.

It was precisely the weightless vision that appealed to his Western readers, whose own dissatisfaction he shared, or for whom he served as representative and interpreter. "Neurasthenic" himself—to use a common term of his age—or at least given to a variety of personal and physical ailments, he could carry the hopes of others similarly inflicted, the hundreds of thousands of contemporaries in the West who looked with foreboding on their own civilized or overcivilized world and who, as Stefan Zweig suggested, could read Hearn as if his books were themselves almost a visit to Japan. When Hearn's often mannered (if highly personal) style became dated, and when Japan emerged as a major power rather than a potential escape for Western visitors, the popularity of the Japanese books naturally declined, remaining strong only among

the Japanese themselves, for whom Hearn kindled a historical longing and a flattering, if outdated, way to see themselves.

Hearn's reputation took a peculiar course. Many of
his books were crowded into the last years of his life or
appeared after his death, with the result that most European editions were posthumous. Recognized during his
lifetime, his popularity in the West actually peaked after
1904. Thirteen editions of his individual works appeared
in both France and Germany, and there were scattered editions in Sweden, Holland, Italy, Spain, and Russia.[33] At
first there were few Japanese editions of his works, in either language, but, as the years passed, the Japanese published more and more of his books, including omnibus
collections of works written prior to his years in Japan. The
Japanese publisher Hokuseido continued where Houghton
Mifflin left off. (Later Charles E. Tuttle Publishers brought
out reprints of Hearn's Japanese books in the United States
and Japan.)

The fate of Hearn's reputation suggests one final perspective on his life and work. I quoted above a comment by
James Clifford in his historical overview of ethnography
and "ethnographic authority." Clifford describes the growth
of ethnographic authority from nineteenth-century origins through its heyday with Bronislaw Malinowski, Margaret Mead, and A. R. Radcliffe-Brown.[34] The failings and
strengths of the field competed from the outset. Ethnography relied heavily on unstated assumptions about cultural difference and otherness, with the Western and self-
consciously civilized outsiders immersing themselves in a
primitive or exotic culture. In the shift from missionary
and other "field-workers" to on-the-spot observation by
the ethnographer him- or herself, the person who could
best show that "I was there" became the person with the
greatest sympathy, the greatest patience, the greatest appreciation for that other culture, the language and mores of
which he actually lived as well as observed.

When, in her early biography of Hearn, Elizabeth Bisland

sought to characterize his gifts, she contrasted him with writers such as Isabella Bird, dismissing Bird as a mere "ethnographer." Hearn, by contrast, was less limited by a scientific spirit, more attuned to the life of the culture. Yet Hearn himself spoke highly of genuine ethnography and, as early as 1885, bemoaned the fact that British travelers lacked ethnographic ability and training.[35] His delight in Japan's difference, his reliance on the applications of Spencer's theories, and his recurrent if hesitant sense that, as the best witness, he was the best commentator, all speak to the assumptions behind ethnographic fieldwork of the sort Franz Boas was pioneering. If he did not (any more than many trained ethnographers) master the language of the culture he studied, he certainly managed to see behind appearances, to appreciate the importance of Shinto and Buddhist beliefs and the relationship between historic patterns and present trends. He failed to realize the implications of Japan's growing nationalism, with its imperialistic ends, and he may not have grasped the centrality of capital to Japan's advancing industrialization—no doubt because temperamentally he would have preferred no industrialization. Nor did he, *Japan* excepted, have enough "constructive ability" to write sustained arguments (however much his books attained, as he might have said, organic wholes.)[36] Yet maybe no one offered readers sharper or more poignant or insightful images or made those images signs of larger patterns in the society.

If these explanations make sense, they do not touch the larger question as to why Hearn and Hearn alone became so preeminent, so persuasive a spokesman, in the late nineteenth and early twentieth centuries. Hearn's modesty rarely allowed him to admit his power or his influence. Did he not see that he eclipsed writers like Chamberlain, who may in the long run have been even more partial to Japan? Did he not wonder why his voice was stronger than Fenollosa's or Loti's or that of any number of ambitious reporters of Eastern experiences? The Japanese still honor Hearn, perhaps more than they honor Fenollosa, who received an astonishing tribute after his death: his remains were brought back to Japan on a Japanese warship. Fenollosa and Hearn would both be remembered by a different Japan as cultural conservers—and as signposts to an era long dead. Hearn may be remembered with the most meaningful sort of posterity: His books are still read, his tributes to the country still appreciated by the Japanese, albeit there is some question about whether, with his works no longer required reading, Hearn is known by a younger generation.[37] In any case, what other non-Western country so remembers a foreign commentator? How many literary figures of any nationality receive the honors paid to Hearn on the centenary of his arrival in Japan?

Creating something of a new genre in and about a new land, Hearn's expansive self (or, as he would put it, selves) invited readers to take their own imaginative journeys. Appreciative of his friend's many talents, Basil Hall Chamberlain quoted from a letter he had received from one of Hearn's admirers; it says much about Hearn's writing: "He is not like Sir Edwin Arnold. He does not do it [write] from a vulgar wish to show off superior knowledge. . . . He really knows. But I wish he would have condescended more to us who don't know."[38] But Hearn was never certain that he did know and thus could not, with honesty, "condescend" to others. So often in his letters he speaks of himself as inadequate, gaining, as he put it, "by disillusion,"[39] lacking new creative energies, or writing poorly— or at least not writing with the passion or precision of a Kipling. With few friends and little reassurance, it must have been extremely difficult to remain confident of his abilities, the more so because he did not write fiction and poetry. He could, with integrity, say, "You are here, because I am here."

"It is hard," Ruth Benedict wrote, "to be conscious of the eyes through which one looks."[40] Hearn more than most writers was conscious, almost pathologically conscious, of his wounded eyes and the way he saw. He scrutinized himself through the various stages of his life, writing letters

that are full of wit and confession while using his correspondents as physicians for his maladies. Related qualities
carry over into his published writings. His chameleon
temperament—or at least ever-shifting moods—allowed
him to move from evocations of horror to plaintive and
nostalgic tales, from precise daily details to dramatic public scenes, from ordinary men and women to the heroes of
yesterday or the ghosts of the night. This "creature of extremes," in his own phrase, projected a world of extremes
for those who encountered—and who still encounter—his
works.

Did Hearn portray the real Japan in those dozen books
from *Glimpses* to *Romance of the Milky Way?* Fascinated
by everything from the "funny little things" of day-to-day
life to the religious and economic substructures of the society, he looked with care and curiosity. But, of course, he
described "a fictive nation," in Roland Barthes's words, a
faraway system of his own realizing, which Hearn, the
chronic namer, called "Japan." True, but no less true that
the "moments of being" he watched so closely and drew so
well for others speak to a shared fiction or connect with
what Hearn himself would have argued to be a collective
reality. There can be, he insisted, no absolute truth; there
can be an indefinable but no less genuine common bond.
The sad irony in Hearn's case is that the world he shared
grew out of profound loneliness, out of a painful need for
love and sympathy. I think of the swimmer, disappearing
from the coast, possibly frightened but less frightened than
excited by the unknown, dreaming of Urashima or ancient
Greece or his "first day in the Orient," a swimmer with a
rare destiny and a matchless talent.

Notes

Preface

Epigraph: Quoted in Elizabeth Bisland, *Life and Letters of Lafcadio Hearn*, 2 vols. (Boston: Houghton Mifflin, 1906), reprinted in *The Writings of Lafcadio Hearn*, 16 vols. (Boston: Houghton Mifflin, 1922), 13:294.

1. Stefan Zweig, intro., *Das Japanbuch, Eine Auswahl aus Hearn's Werken* (Frankfurt am Main: Rütten and Loening, 1911), 1. See Kathleen W. Webb's informative *Lafcadio Hearn and His German Critics: An Examination of His Appeal* (New York: Peter Lang, 1984).

2. See Michael Shapiro's engaging autobiographical account, *Japan: In the Land of the Brokenhearted* (New York: Henry Holt, 1989), which plays off the author's experiences against the memory of Hearn.

3. Carl Dawson, *Prophets of Past Time: Seven British Autobiographers, 1880–1914* (Baltimore: Johns Hopkins University Press, 1988).

4. Nordau's notorious book appeared in English in 1895 (New York: D. Appleton) and was read for the next generation.

5. Hearn, *Japan: An Attempt at Interpretation* (1904), *Writings*, 12:444.

6. Hearn, letter to the Henry Alden family, 17 June 1888, *New Hearn Letters from the French West Indies*, ed. Ichiro Nishizaki, reprinted from *Studies in Arts and Culture* (Ochanomizu University, Tokyo) (June 1959): 79.

7. Herbert Spencer called his system the "synthetic philosophy." See, for example, *An Autobiography* (New York: D. Appleton, 1904); and *First Principles* (New York: A. L. Burt, 1880).

8. George M. Gould, *Concerning Lafcadio Hearn*, with a bibliography by Laura Stedman (Philadelphia: George Jacobs, 1908), 4.

9. Hearn, letter of 1885 to W. D. O'Connor, cited in *Leaves from the Diary of an Impressionist: Early Writings of Lafcadio Hearn*, ed. Ferris Greenslet (Boston: Houghton Mifflin, 1911), 21.

10. Paul Elmer More, "Lafcadio Hearn," *Atlantic Monthly* (February 1903): 204, reprinted in *Selected Shelburne Essays* (New York: Oxford University Press, 1935), 25–46.

11. Douglas Cole, " 'The Value of a Person Lies in his *Herzensbildung*': Franz Boas' Baffin Island Letter Diary, 1883–1884," in *Observers Ob-*

served: Essays on Ethnographic Fieldwork, ed. George W. Stocking, Jr., History of Anthropology Series (Madison: University of Wisconsin Press, 1983), 1:40.

12. See Edward Said, *Orientalism* (New York: Pantheon, 1978). I have used the 1979 Vintage edition in subsequent references.

13. See Albert Mordell's introduction to *Lafcadio Hearn: An American Miscellany: Articles and Studies Now First Collected* [from newspaper articles] (New York: Dodd, Mead, 1924), in which Mordell describes his search for Hearn's uncollected writings. Punctuation, he suggests, identifies many of the articles along with Hearn's overuse of words such as *ghostly, grotesque, lurid,* and *atrocious.*

14. Jonathan Cott's *Wandering Ghost: The Odyssey of Lafcadio Hearn* (New York: Alfred A. Knopf, 1990) appeared shortly after my book had gone to the publisher; I was, therefore, unable to make use of its extensive research. I was also unable to consult *A General Catalogue of Hearn Collections in Japan and Overseas*, comp. Kenji Zenimoto (Matsue: The Hearn Society, 1991).

15. The paperback editions are published by Charles E. Tuttle, Publishers.

1. The Voyage Out

Epigraphs: Walt Whitman, "Facing West from California," *Leaves of Grass: Comprehensive Reader's Edition*, ed. Harold W. Blodgett and Sculley Bradley (New York: New York University Press, 1965), 111; Ernest Francisco Fenollosa, *The Masters of Ukiyoe: A Complete Historical Description* [a catalog] (New York: W. H. Ketcham, 1896), 100.

1. See especially Hearn, *Exotics and Retrospectives* (1898; reprint, Rutland, Vt.: Charles E. Tuttle, 1971).

2. *Nation* 59, no. 1532, 346.

3. Hearn, *A History of English Literature*, 2 vols., ed. R. Tanabe, T. Ochiai, I. Nishizaki (1927; reprint, Tokyo: Hokuseido, 1953), 2:772.

4. Roland Barthes, *Empire of Signs*, trans. Richard Howard (New York: Hill and Wang, 1982), 4.

5. Quoted in Elizabeth Stevenson, *Lafcadio Hearn* (New York: Macmillan, 1961), 194.

6. Hearn, letter to Basil Hall Chamberlain, 16 May 1894, *Japanese Letters, Writings*, 16:185.

7. John La Farge, *An Artist's Letters from Japan* (New York: Century, 1897); also *John La Farge*, essays by Henry Adams, Kathleen A. Foster, et al. (New York: Abbeville, 1987). For Beato's photographs, see, for example, *Japan: Photographs, 1854–1905*, ed. Clark Worswick, intro. Jan Morris (New York: Alfred A. Knopf, 1979).

8. See Harry E. Wedeck, *Mortal Hunger: A Novel Based on the Life of Lafcadio Hearn* (New York: Sheridan, 1947); and Dennis Rose, *Lafcadio*

Hearn: His Sun Was Dark (Lewes, Sussex: Book Guild, 1987). Neither work does Hearn much justice. In addition to Stevenson's biography, see, among others, Bisland, *Life and Letters,* in *Writings,* vol. 13; Nina H. Kennard, *Lafcadio Hearn* (London: E. Nash, 1911); Edward Larocque Tinker, *Lafcadio Hearn's American Days* (New York: Dodd, Mead, 1924); Jean Temple, *Blue Ghost: A Study of Lafcadio Hearn* (New York: Jonathan Cape, 1931); Vera Seeley McWilliams, *Lafcadio Hearn* (Boston: Houghton Mifflin, 1946); O. W. Frost, *Young Hearn* (Tokyo: Hokuseido, 1958); Robert A. Rosenstone, *Mirror in the Shrine: American Encounters with Meiji Japan* (Cambridge: Harvard University Press, 1988); Cott, *Wandering Ghost.*

9. *Detroit Times,* 18 August 1933, 10.

10. Malcolm Cowley, intro., *The Selected Writings of Lafcadio Hearn,* ed. Henry Goodman (New York: Citadel, 1949), 2.

11. Lafcadio Hearn, undated letter (probably from 1889 or early 1890), "Letters of Lafcadio Hearn to His Brother," ed. E. C. Beck, *English Journal* 20 (1931): 288.

12. See the autobiographical fragments, reprinted in *Life and Letters, Writings,* 13:15–44; and the letters to his half-sister, Minnie Atkinson, scattered throughout Kennard's *Lafcadio Hearn.*

13. Hearn, *Out of the East: Reveries and Studies in New Japan* (1895; reprint, Rutland, Vt.: Charles E. Tuttle, 1972), 20.

14. *Writings,* 13:17–24. Ferris Greenslet suggests that Hearn's finished autobiography might well have proven to be his best work (*Diary of an Impressionist,* 27–28). In fact, all of his work is a form of autobiography, though he was unwilling or unable to remember many episodes from his boyhood and youth.

15. The chronology is debated. See Albert Mordell, *Discoveries: Essays on Lafcadio Hearn* (Tokyo: Orient/West, 1964), 4.

16. Hearn, "Hi-Mawari," *Kwaidan: Stories and Studies of Strange Things* (1904; reprint, Rutland, Vt.: Charles E. Tuttle, 1971).

17. *Note-Books* (Case 27), C. Waller Barrett Collection, 6101, Alderman Library, University of Virginia (hereafter referred to as "Barrett"). At various times Hearn speaks of several disabling injuries, especially to his back, which kept him bedridden for months.

18. Bisland, *Life and Letters, Writings,* 13:34.

19. See John Ball, intro., *Children of the Levee,* ed. O. W. Frost (Lexington: University of Kentucky Press, 1957), 1.

20. Letter to Chamberlain, 25 November 1893, in Barrett.

21. See *Letters from the Raven: Being the Correspondence of Lafcadio Hearn with Henry Watkin,* ed. Milton Bronner (New York: Brentano's, 1907).

22. This article, "Violent Cremation," which is reprinted in Mordell's collection, appeared in the Cincinnati *Enquirer,* 9 November 1874. See Jon Christopher Hughes, *The Tanyard Murder: On the Case*

with *Lafcadio Hearn* (Washington, D.C.: University Press of America, 1982).

23. See Mordell, intro., *American Miscellany*, with its information from Edwin Henderson, Hearn's editor, on the *Commercial*, and other contemporaries.

24. Several collections of these writings have been published in book form, including Ball, *Children of the Levee*. See also Mordell, *American Miscellany;* and *The New Radiance, and Other Scientific Sketches*, and *Barbarous Barbers and Other Stories*, both ed. Ichiro Nishizaki (Tokyo: Hokuseido, 1939). See also the new edition of *Period of the Gruesome: Selected Cincinnati Journalism of Lafcadio Hearn*, ed. Jon Christopher Hughes (Lanham, Md.: University Press of America, 1990).

25. Cincinnati *Enquirer*, 21 December 1873, quoted in Stevenson, *Lafcadio Hearn*, 38.

26. "Some Strange Experience: The Reminiscences of a Ghost-Seer," Cincinnati *Commercial*, 26 September 1875, reprinted in Mordell, *American Miscellany*, 62.

27. "Two Unpublished Hearn Letters," ed. O. W. Frost, *Today's Japan* 5, no. 1 (January 1960): 45.

28. Quoted in Oscar Lewis, *Hearn and His Biographers: The Record of a Literary Controversy* (San Francisco: Westgate Press, 1930), 53–54.

29. Hearn, *La Cuisine Creole: A Collection of Culinary Recipes* (1885; reprint, New York: Penguin, 1990); *"Gombo Zhèbes": Little Dictionary of Creole Proverbs, Selected from Six Creole Dialects* (New York: W. H. Coleman, 1885).

30. Edward Larocque Tinker, "Lafcadio Hearn, Columnist and Cartoonist," *New York Times Magazine* (13 April 1924): 6. Hearn also wrote for the New Orleans *Times-Democrat*. Among his translations, see Gautier, *One of Cleopatra's Nights, and Other Fantastic Romances* (New York: R. Worthington, 1882).

31. See the collection of Hearn's commentary, *Editorials* [from the *Item* and *Times-Democrat*], ed. Charles Woodward Hutson (Boston: Houghton Mifflin, 1926).

32. Hearn, *Chita: A Memory of Last Island* (New York: Harper and Brothers, 1889).

33. "Letters of a Poet to a Musician: Letters from Hearn to H. E. Krehbiel," *Critic* (April 1906): 48–49.

34. "Newly Discovered Letters from Lafcadio Hearn to Dr. Rudolph Matas," ed. Ichiro Nishizaki, *Ochanomizu University Studies* (Tokyo) 8 (March 1965): 85. Matas's collection provided the basis of the repository of Hearn materials at the Howard-Tilton Memorial Library.

35. Hearn, *Youma: The Story of a West-Indian Slave* (New York: Harper and Brothers, 1890).

36. Letter to the Henry Alden family, 17 July 1888, *New Hearn Letters from the French West Indies*, 78.

37. See Mordell's informed praise of Hearn in *Discoveries.* Mordell objects to Stevenson and others calling Hearn "minor": "We have in Hearn . . . the greatest descriptive writer and the greatest prose poet in America" (225).

38. Hearn, *Two Years in the French West Indies* (New York: Harper and Brothers, 1890); *Glimpses of Unfamiliar Japan,* 2 vols. (1894; reprint, Rutland, Vt.: Charles E. Tuttle, 1976).

39. "Newly Discovered Letters," 117.

40. Letter to O'Connor, March 1885, *Writings,* 13:340.

41. See especially Gould, *Concerning Lafcadio Hearn.*

42. Letter of 7–8 March 1890, *Writings,* 13:470–75.

43. "Newly Discovered Letters," 90. Bisland, as Hearn anticipated, achieved success as a writer. She wrote novels, political pamphlets (against war), and other books on diverse topics, including an account of a trip around the world. She did not see Hearn on her brief visit to Japan.

44. Bisland, *Life and Letters, Writings,* 13:73.

45. Hearn, article from 27 June 1878, *Editorials,* 6.

46. This was part of a proposal for *Harper's Magazine,* quoted in Tinker, *Lafcadio Hearn's American Days,* 328–29.

47. Hearn, "Winter Journey to Japan," *Harper's Magazine* 81, no. 486 (November 1890), reprinted in *Lands and Seas,* ed. T. Ochiai (Tokyo: Hokuseido, 1925).

48. *Buying Christmas Toys and Other Essays* (Tokyo: Hokuseido, 1939), 32.

49. Quoted in Said, *Orientalism,* 167, who says: "One always returned to the Orient."

50. Letter to Ernest Francisco Fenollosa, 13 April 1890, *Writings,* 13:28. Quoted in Lawrence W. Chisolm, *Fenollosa: the Far East and American Culture* (New Haven: Yale University Press, 1963), 147.

51. *Out of the East,* 20.

52. Yone Noguchi, "A Conversation with Mrs. Lafcadio Hearn," *Japan Times,* 21 December 1904, 6.

53. Herbert Marcuse, *The Aesthetic Dimension: Toward a Critique of Marxist Aesthetics* (Boston: Beacon Press, 1978), 73.

54. Oscar Lewis, "Letters of Lafcadio Hearn to Joseph Tunison," in *Hearn and His Biographers: The Record of a Literary Controversy* (San Francisco: Westgate Press, 1930), 9, 11.

55. McDonald not only retained Hearn's friendship through the final years; he also became a dedicated and resourceful literary executor, providing materials and urging publication for many posthumous volumes. He died in the great Tokyo earthquake of 1923.

56. Sadasaburo Ochiai, in *Stenographic Records of the Round-Table Meeting of Reminiscences of the Late Lafcadio Hearn* (29 March 1940), sponsored by the Society for International Cultural Relations, comp. P. D. Perkins, 58; cited in the *National Union Catalogue* but available in type-

script only. I have used copies in the Barrett Collection and the Howard-Tilton Library, Tulane University.

57. See the account by Kazuo Koizumi, Hearn's son, of Hearn and Chamberlain in his foreword to *Letters from Basil Hall Chamberlain to Lafcadio Hearn* (Tokyo: Hokuseido, 1936): "The gentlemen fully understood Hearn's disposition and temperament, and kept him in favor to the last" (i).

58. Letter to Page M. Baker, January 1896, *Writings*, 15:14.

59. At the 1990 centennial festival commemorating Hearn's arrival in Matsue, Professor Yuzo Ota argued persuasively that Chamberlain was a more consistent commentator on Japan and perhaps less biased than Hearn. This is debatable, given expressions such as "English as she is Japped," the title of a chapter in Chamberlain's *Japanese Things* [later *Things Japanese*]: *Being Notes on Various Subjects Connected with Japan* (1890; reprint, Rutland, Vt.: Charles E. Tuttle, 1971).

60. Rosenstone makes this observation, contrasting the published book with a private letter Hearn wrote to Chamberlain, in *Mirror in the Shrine*, 49–50.

61. See Francis King's insightful introduction to *Lafcadio Hearn: Writings from Japan: An Anthology* (Harmondsworth, Middlesex: Penguin, 1984), 11.

62. Letter to Hearn from Sentarō Nishida, n.d., in Barrett.

63. *Glimpses*, 691–92, 693.

64. Details of the relationship, including when and where they married, remain obscure. See Yoji Hasegawa, *Lafcadio Hearn's Japanese Wife: Her Memoirs and Her Early Life* (Tokyo: Microprinting, 1988), 109–15.

65. Letter to Ellwood Hendrick, September 1895, *Writings*, 14:384–85.

66. Independent Japanese who, at great peril, went or tried to go abroad intrigued Hearn and other Westerners. See, for example, the story by Robert Louis Stevenson (a writer Hearn admired), "Yoshida Turajiro," about another Choshu samurai, who called for reforms and tried to stow away on Commodore Perry's ships (*Familiar Studies of Men and Books* [New York: Scribner's, 1904]). Hearn read with pleasure Stevenson's South Sea books, especially *The Wrecker* (1892).

67. See, for example, Edwin O. Reischauer, *The Japanese* (Cambridge: Belknap Press of Harvard University Press, 1981), 2d ed., 88–93, for a brief survey of the Meiji Restoration; and W. G. Beasley, *The Meiji Restoration* (Stanford: Stanford University Press, 1972), for a fuller account.

68. B. H. Chamberlain and W. B. Mason, *A Handbook for Travellers in Japan* (1891; reprint, London: John Murray, 1913).

69. For a discussion of the almost inevitable imperialism inherent in Japan's nationalistic development, see, for example, Benedict Anderson's *Imagined Communities: Reflections on the Origin and Spread of Nationalism* (London: Verso, 1983), esp. 92–93.

70. Sir G. B. Sansom, *The Western World and Japan: A Study of the*

Interaction of European and Asiatic Countries (1949; reprint, Rutland, Vt.: Charles E. Tuttle, 1987).

71. See Toshio Yokoyama, *Japan in the Victorian Mind: A Study of the Stereotyped Image of a Nation, 1850–1880* (London: Macmillan, 1987).

72. Setsuko Koizumi [Mrs. Hearn], *Reminiscences of Lafcadio Hearn*, trans. Paul Kyoshi Hisada and Frederick Johnson (Boston: Houghton Mifflin, 1918), 31.

73. Letter to Chamberlain, 26 January 1894, *Writings*, 16:103.

74. Setsuko Koizumi, *Reminiscences*, 31. She adds that "he avoided society and seemed eccentric because he valued so highly things of beauty" (33).

75. On Hearn's apparent suicide attempt in Cincinnati, see Stevenson, *Lafcadio Hearn*, 54–55.

76. See, for example, *Karma and Other Stories and Essays*, ed. Albert Mordell (New York: Boni and Liveright, 1918).

77. See his wife's remark in *Reminiscences:* "When he simply heard the name 'Urashima,' he exclaimed aloud, saying, 'Ah! Urashima!'" (59).

78. *Out of the East*, 7.

79. *Glimpses*, 692.

80. Sigmund Freud, *Civilization and Its Discontents*, in *Standard Edition of the Complete Psychological Works*, ed. and trans. James Strachey, 24 vols. (1953; reprint, London: Hogarth Press, 1978), 21:64. On different aspects of Freud, see Mordell's "Hearn Foresaw Views of Freud," review of Temple's *Blue Ghost, Philadelphia Record*, 3 January 1931.

81. *Out of the East*, 11.

82. Hearn, "Notes of a Trip to Izumo," *Atlantic Monthly* 79 (May 1897): 680.

83. Letter to Mason, 28 May 1892, *Writings*, 16:303.

84. Letter to Nishida, 1891, *Writings*, 14:169.

85. Letters to Chamberlain, 17 July 1894 and 18 May 1894, *Writings*, 16:222, 185.

86. Letter to Chamberlain, 30 May 1893, *Writings*, 16:423.

87. *Out of the East*, 325.

88. Lafcadio Hearn, letter to Nishida, 8 July 1894, *Some New Letters and Writings of Lafcadio Hearn*, ed. Sanki Ichikawa (Tokyo: Kenkyusha, 1925), 120.

89. Letter to W. B. Mason, 1892?, *Writings*, 16:314–15.

90. *History of English Literature*, 2:632.

2. Western Writers in Japan

Epigraph: Quoted by Nobushige Amenomori, the Japanese friend Hearn perhaps most admired, in his insightful "Lafcadio Hearn, the Man," *Atlantic Monthly* 96 (October 1905): 520.

1. Chamberlain, *Japanese Things,* 68, 70. For a discussion of Western responses to Japan in the pre-Hearn years, see Toshio Yokoyama's informative *Japan in the Victorian Mind.* For a discussion of Japanese responses to the West, see Masao Miyoshi's *As We Saw Them: The First Japanese Embassy to the United States (1860)* (Berkeley: University of California Press, 1979).

2. Chamberlain, *Japanese Things,* 70, 3. Hearn very much admired Sir Edwin Arnold's popular *The Light of Asia; or The Great Renunciation* (1879), a narrative about the Buddha. For more on Lawrence Oliphant, who also wrote political analyses, see, for example, "The Moral and Political Revolution in Japan," *Blackwood's Magazine* 101 (1867): 427–43.

3. See André Fermigier, *Pierre Bonnard* (New York: Abrams, 1984), 14–15.

4. See, for example, Siegfried Wichmann, *Japonisme: The Japanese Influence on Western Art in the Nineteenth and Twentieth Centuries,* trans. Mary Whitall et al. (New York: Harmony Books, 1981); and Klaus Berger, *Japonismus in der westlichen Malerei, 1860–1920* (Munich: H. Prestel Verlag, 1980).

5. Said, *Orientalism,* 181. See also Raymond Schwab, *The Oriental Renaissance: Europe's Rediscovery of India and the East, 1680–1880,* trans. Gene Patterson-Black and Victor Reinking (New York: Columbia University Press, 1984).

6. See Jan Morris's essay in Worswick's *Japan: Photographs,* 8.

7. *The Enigma of Japanese Power: People and Politics in a Stateless Nation* is Karel van Wolferen's title for a book he describes as "the first full-scale examination of Japan's political-industrial system" (New York: Alfred A. Knopf, 1989).

8. Hearn, *Some Chinese Ghosts* (Boston: Roberts Brothers, 1887), *Writings,* 1:217.

9. See the discussion of Herbert Spencer in Ronald E. Martin, *American Literature and the Universe of Force* (Durham, N.C.: Duke University Press, 1981), esp. 32–58.

10. *Writings,* 1:287.

11. Letter to Mason, 6 August 1892, *Writings,* 16:290.

12. In his witty *Abroad: British Literary Traveling between the Wars* (New York: Oxford, 1980), Paul Fussell associates tourism with the twentieth century and contrasts its mechanical decadence with earlier "travel." In fact, tourism had been satirized and was a thriving way of life long before World War I.

13. Clara A. N. Whitney, *Clara's Diary: An American Girl in Meiji Japan,* ed. M. William Steele and Tamiko Ichimata (Tokyo: Kodansha, 1981). Whitney's accounts of the family's struggles and of her own personal problems (she entered into an unhappy marriage with a Japanese man) both corroborate and undercut Hearn's criticisms.

14. Letter of May 1899, *Writings,* 15:179.

15. Hearn, *A Japanese Miscellany* (1901; reprint, Rutland, Vt.: Charles E. Tuttle, 1967), 238.

16. Letter to Chamberlain, 28 June 1894, in Barrett. On William Elliott Griffis, see Edward R. Beauchamp, *An American Teacher in Early Meiji Japan* (Honolulu: University Press of Hawaii, 1976).

17. See, for example, William Elliott Griffis, *Japan: Its History, Folklore and Art* (Boston: Houghton Mifflin, 1892), a delightful account for young readers and one of a dozen books Griffis wrote about Japan. Others include *The Mikado's Empire* (New York: Harper and Brothers, 1900), *The Japanese Nation in Evolution* (New York: Crowell, 1907), and several books about the United States' role in the East.

18. Rosenstone, *Mirror in the Shrine*, esp. the chapter "Seductive Temptations."

19. Griffis wrote a favorable review of Hearn's posthumous *The Romance of the Milky Way, and Other Studies and Stories* (1905), in *Critic* (6 March 1906): 222.

20. Algernon Bertram Freeman-Mitford, Lord Redesdale, *Mitford's Japan: The Memoirs and Recollections, 1866–1906*, ed. Hugh Cortazzi (London: Athlone, 1985), 56.

21. Hugh Cortazzi, ed., *Dr. Willis in Japan, 1862–1877: British Medical Pioneer* (London: Athlone, 1985), 1–3.

22. An otherwise appreciative notice in the *Saturday Review* ([11 March 1871]: 317–18) dismisses Mitford's claim to offer a complete view of Japanese civilization. Folklore, the writer says, can only serve this function when a civilization is more advanced than that of Japan.

23. See chap. 6, "Hearn and Japanese Civilization."

24. Letter to Chamberlain, 6 March 1894, *Writings*, 16:141.

25. Isabella L. Bird, *Unbeaten Tracks in Japan*, intro. Pat Barr (1880; reprint, Boston: Beacon Press, 1987), 1, 81. Another impressive book by a female visitor is the Philadelphian Anna C. Hartshorne's *Japan and Her People*, 2 vols. (Philadelphia: Henry T. Coates, 1902). Hartshorne lived in Japan and wrote sympathetically about its "everyday life." Her book may have appeared a little late for Hearn to have read it.

26. Letter of 16 August 1893, *Some New Letters*, 100.

27. Setsuko Koizumi, *Reminiscences*, in Yone Noguchi, *Lafcadio Hearn in Japan* (London: Kelly and Walsh, 1910), 48.

28. It is, however, Hearn who speaks favorably of "Dr. Tylor, the great anthropologist" (letter of 27 June 1892, *Some New Letters*, 32). In *More Letters from Basil Hall Chamberlain to Lafcadio Hearn* Chamberlain speaks of sending some of Hearn's descriptions of Japan to Tylor ([Tokyo: Hokuseido, 1937], 10).

29. Long before going to Japan, Hearn was already using terms such as *ethnography* to dismiss the narrowness of English travelers (letter to Henry E. Krehbiel, 1885, *Writings*, 13:334).

30. Quoted in *Stories from Pierre Loti*, trans. Lafcadio Hearn, intro.

Albert Mordell (Tokyo: Hokuseido, 1933), vi. See among other late collections, *Sketches and Tales from the French*, ed. Mordell (Tokyo: Hokuseido, 1935).

31. See Bisland, *Life and Letters*, in *Writings*, 13:374. Hearn's translations can be found in *Stories from Pierre Loti*.

32. See Hearn's translation of "A Love Match in Tahiti," New Orleans *Times-Democrat*, 17 October 1880, reprinted in *Stories from Pierre Loti*, which deals briefly with another such "marriage."

33. Letter to Mason, 30 July 1892, *Writings*, 16:281.

34. Pierre Loti, *Madame Chrysanthème* (1888), trans. Laura Ensor (Paris: Edouard Guillaume, 1989), 242.

35. Loti, *Madame Chrysanthème*, 198, 14–15, 216.

36. David Belasco wrote the play *Madame Butterfly*, based on John Luther Long's story (which was published in 1898); it first appeared in March 1900 in New York (and was later made into a film starring Cary Grant). On Puccini, see Mosco Carner, *Puccini: a Critical Biography* (London: Duckworth, 1958), 125–29.

37. Pierre Loti, *Japoneries d'Automne*, quoted in *Once Upon a Time: Visions of Old Japan from the Photos of Beato and Stillfried and the Words of Pierre Loti*, intro. Chantal Edel, trans. Linda Coverdale (New York: Friendly Press, 1986), 4. Edel speaks of Loti's "unabashed worship" of the empress.

38. Quoted in Caroline Ticknor, *Glimpses of Authors* (Boston: Houghton Mifflin, 1922), 123.

39. See, for example, Hearn, *Kotto: Being Japanese Curios, with Sundry Cobwebs* (1902; reprint, Rutland, Vt.: Charles E. Tuttle, 1971), 210: "The more that races evolve towards higher things, the more Feminine becomes their idea of God."

40. Photocopies distributed by Yasuyuki Kajitani, in "Some Considerations on Lafcadio Hearn in Matsue" (Paper presented at the Hearn Centennial Conference in Matsue, Japan, 2 September 1990). Professor Kajitani has written extensively about Hearn in Japan. See, for example, "Some New Materials and Investigation concerning Lafcadio Hearn's Matsue Days," *Journal of Shimane University* (1961) 10: 1–19 and 11: 1–31.

41. Hearn, *Notebook*, 1890–91, in Barrett, 43–44. See a modern and parallel, though more ironic, discussion of a similar encounter in Bernard Rudofsky's *The Kimono Mind: An Informal Guide to Japan and the Japanese* (1965; reprint, New York: Van Nostrand Reinhold, 1982), 36–39.

42. See Letter of July 1887 to Rudolph Matas, "Newly Discovered Letters," 88.

43. Hearn's interest in race, as mentioned above, prompted his studies of African Americans in Cincinnati, Creoles in New Orleans, and the mixed peoples of the Caribbean. See especially Ball, *Children of the*

Levee, and Hearn's letters to Matas from Martinique in "Newly Discovered Letters."

44. Donald Keene, in *Japan Times,* 6 April 1988, 16.

45. Loti, *Madame Chrysanthème.*

46. Hearn, letter to Chamberlain, 18 February 1893, *Writings,* 16:329.

47. See, for example, Kurt Singer, *Mirror, Sword, and Jewel: A Study of Japanese Characteristics,* intro. Richard Storry (New York: George Braziller, 1973), esp. 46–48, "The Mists of Concealment."

48. Letter to Mason, 1 November 1892, *Writings,* 16:312–13.

49. Letter to Chamberlain, 18 February 1893, *Writings,* 16:61.

50. Loti, *Madame Chrysanthème,* 171–72.

51. Letter to Mason, 1 November 1892, *Writings,* 16:313.

52. Hearn, "At a Railway Station," *Kokoro: Hints and Echoes of Japanese Inner Life* (1896; reprint, Rutland, Vt.: Charles E. Tuttle, 1972), 4.

53. Letter to Chamberlain, 31 October 1893, *Writings,* 16:60. *Yoshiwara* was the ancient pleasure district of Yedo (Tokyo). Among other studies, see Stephen and Ethel Longstreet, *Yoshiwara: the Pleasure Quarters of Old Tokyo* (Rutland, Vt.: Charles E. Tuttle, 1988).

54. Undated letter to Mason (1892?), *Writings* 16:314–16. In the same letter he complains about Kipling's cynicism and hardness but still thinks him a "colossus."

55. Letter to Mason, 1892, *Writings,* 16:316.

56. Rudyard Kipling, *Kipling's Japan: Collected Writings,* ed. Hugh Cortazzi and George Webb (Atlantic Highlands, N.J.: Athlone Press, 1988), 7.

57. *Kipling's Japan,* 54.

58. Hearn, *Glimpses,* 5–6. Interestingly, when Hearn writes for an audience of Westerners in Japan he shares Kipling's reduction of the rickshaw drivers, about whose predatory habits he warns his readers. See "The Kurumaya Question," *Editorials from the Kobe "Chronicle,"* ed. Makoto Sangu (Tokyo: Hokuseido, 1960), 5–7.

59. Chamberlain, *Things Japanese;* quoted in *Kipling's Japan,* x.

60. For an assessment of Kipling as entirely sympathetic to Japan and open to its special qualities, see Earl R. Miner, *The Japanese Tradition in British and American Literature* (Princeton: Princeton University Press, 1958), 33–35.

61. "Kipling at the Tokyo Club" (7 May 1892), in *Kipling's Japan,* 226.

62. Van Wyck Brooks, *Fenollosa and his Circle, with Other Essays in Biography* (New York: E. P. Dutton, 1962), 1–68. See also his "Lafcadio Hearn in Japan," *The Confident Years, 1885–1915* (New York: E. P. Dutton, 1952).

63. See, for example, Hearn, "Japanese Civilization," in *Kokoro,* 18–21. In *The Pleasures of Japanese Literature* (New York: Columbia University Press, 1988) Donald Keene isolates four essential principles of Japanese aesthetics: *suggestion, irregularity, simplicity,* and *perishability.* Hearn

himself appreciated Japanese art in these terms.

64. Cited in Brooks, *Fenollosa and His Circle*, 41. Both Henry Adams and his friend John La Farge remained cool to Japan, which is understandable in Adams's case, less so in La Farge's, since La Farge had long been influenced by Japanese art.

65. *Stenographic Records*, 2.

66. Hearn, Letter to Fenollosa, 13 April 1890, in Barrett.

67. Hearn was especially irritated by the Japanese government; see his letter to Elizabeth [Bisland] Wetmore, 2 June 1903, *Writings*, 15:230.

68. Ernest Francisco Fenollosa, *The Masters of Ukiyoe: A Complete Historical Description of Japanese Paintings, and Color Prints of the Genre School* (New York: W. H. Ketcham, 1896). Characteristically, Hearn tells Fenollosa (in 1898) that he has lost interest in the now popular ukiyo-e, which "left me cold." Letter of May 1898, *Writings*, 15:115.

69. Quoted in Chisolm, *Fenollosa: The Far East and American Culture*, 140–41.

70. Hearn, letter, 24 August 1888, *Writings*, 13:56.

71. See Bisland, *Writings*, 13:308.

72. Hearn, *Writings*, 13:400–402.

73. Letter to Mason, 30 July 1892, *Writings*, 16:285.

74. He says in a letter to Chamberlain (28 June 1894): "I used to think I had no soul; but since coming here [to Japan] I think I have" (*Writings*, 16:209).

75. When Lowell returned to the United States, he set himself the new mission of understanding Mars and the other planets, and, thanks to his predictions, later astronomers were able to discover the planet Pluto—in 1930, a few years after Lowell's death.

76. Robert S. Ellwood, "Percival Lowell's Journey to the East," *Sewanee Review* 78, no. 2 (1970): 296.

77. Koizumi, *Letters from Chamberlain to Hearn*, 34–35. See, for example, the letter of February 1895 to Chamberlain, *Writings*, 14:319; also letter of 5 August 1893.

78. Percival Lowell, *Occult Japan; or, the Way of the Gods: An Esoteric Study of Japanese Personality and Possession* (Boston: Houghton Mifflin, 1895), 2.

79. Percival Lowell, *The Soul of the Far East* (1888; reprint, New York: Macmillan, 1920), 25.

80. Lowell, *Soul of the Far East*, 8.

81. Hearn, letter to Nishida, 15 April 1896: "The Times and the other English journals have been kind [about his books]." He is, however, "more pleased with the approval of a Japanese friend than with the verdict of a foreign reviewer" (*Writings*, 15:26).

82. Lowell, *Soul of the Far East*, 2.

83. Hearn, "A Living God," *Gleanings in Buddha-Fields: Studies of*

Hand and Soul in the Far East (1897; reprint, Rutland, Vt.: Charles E. Tuttle, 1971), 4–5.

3. The Japanbook

1. Hearn actually lived close to one of his favorite temples in Tokyo and spent time there. See the discussion of the Kobudera temple in "The Literature of the Dead," *Exotics and Retrospectives.*

2. See, for example, Stevenson, *Lafcadio Hearn*, 298–99. Margaret McAdow writes about Hearn's changing styles in *Lafcadio Hearn: A Study of his Literary Development* (Ann Arbor: University Microfilms, 1984).

3. Kenneth Rexroth, ed., *The Buddhist Writings of Lafcadio Hearn* (Santa Barbara: Ross-Erikson, 1977), xi. Hearn offers, he says, "a sensitive and durable vision of how Buddhism was and still is lived in Japan" (vii). Shoko Watanabe argues similarly in a brief article, "Hearn's View of Japanese Buddhism," *Today's Japan* 4 (January 1959): 57–61. On the other hand, Guy Richard Welborn, in his fairly comprehensive *The Buddhist Nirvana and Its Western Interpreters* (Chicago: University of Chicago Press, 1968), fails to mention Hearn at all.

4. Hearn, *Exotics and Retrospectives*, xiii. "Reshaping tales from the Japanese" is Arthur Kunst's apt phrase from *Lafcadio Hearn* (New York: Twayne, 1969), a survey of Hearn's writing career (preface).

5. Albert Camus, *Notebooks, 1935–1942*, trans. Philip Thody (New York: Harcourt Brace Jovanovich, 1978), 11.

6. *Exotics and Retrospectives*, 7.

7. Nina H. Kennard, *Lafcadio Hearn: Containing Some Letters from Lafcadio Hearn to His Half-Sister, Mrs. Atkinson* (1911; reprint, Port Washington, N.Y.: Kennikat, 1967), 281.

8. See Hearn, "New Letters from the French West Indies," 89.

9. *Exotics and Retrospectives*, 4, 6.

10. *Glimpses*, 13.

11. *Exotics and Retrospectives*, 34–35.

12. *Exotics and Retrospectives*, 14.

13. "Violent Cremation," 248. See Jon Christopher Hughes, "The Tanyard Murder," *Dismal Man: Two Radio Plays* (Cincinnati: Poetry Review Press, 1990), 5.

14. *Exotics and Retrospectives*, 36.

15. Letter to Chamberlain, 26 February 1896, in Barrett.

16. *Exotics and Retrospectives*, 22.

17. *Exotics and Retrospectives*, 31.

18. See Julia Kristeva's pertinent *Power of Horror*, trans. Leon Roudiez (New York: Columbia University Press, 1982), which explores meanings of *abjectness.* Kristeva could be speaking of Hearn when she describes

abjection as approaching "a psychic border" where meaning collapses: "Abjection is a state of being neither inside nor outside, neither here nor there" (2).

19. Included in Mordell, *American Miscellany.*

20. *Exotics and Retrospectives,* 16–17.

21. Gaston Bachelard, *The Poetics of Space,* trans. Maria Jolas, foreword by Etienne Gilson (New York: Orion, 1964).

22. Hearn, *Out of the East,* 304, 307.

23. Marcel Robert, *Lafcadio Hearn,* 2 vols. (Tokyo: Hokuseido, 1950–51), translated and published in part as "Lafcadio Hearn," *Transactions of the Asiatic Society of Japan,* 3rd ser. (London: Kegan, Paul, Trench, Trubner, 1948), and as introduction to Hearn, *Selected Writings* (Tokyo: Kenkyusha, 1953), xxvi.

24. Hearn, *Out of the East,* 308–9, 312, 320–21.

25. Hearn's obsession with his own sexuality is clear in the letters to Rudolph Matas, but even Elizabeth Bisland's biographical study includes revealing material on the same topic.

26. Hearn, *Out of the East,* 310.

27. *Out of the East,* 312.

28. *Out of the East,* 314.

29. *Out of the East,* 325.

30. Anthony Storr, *Solitude: A Return to the Self* (New York: Free Press, 1988).

31. "Reminiscences," in Noguchi, *Lafcadio Hearn in Japan,* 76.

32. William Butler Yeats, "Sailing to Byzantium," *Collected Poems* (New York: Macmillan, 1951), 191. On Hearn and Yeats, see Barbara Hayley, *Lafcadio Hearn, William Butler Yeats, and Japan* (Gerrards Cross, Bucks.: Colin Smythe, 1988).

33. Hearn, *In Ghostly Japan* (1899; reprint, Rutland, Vt.: Charles E. Tuttle, 1985), 3.

34. Quoted in Hearn, *Life and Letters, Writings,* 13:140–41.

35. Hearn, *Ghostly Japan,* epigraph.

36. *Ghostly Japan,* 133.

37. *Ghostly Japan,* 135, 136, 137.

38. *Ghostly Japan,* 137–38.

39. *Ghostly Japan,* 140.

40. *Writings,* 13:312.

4. Spirits, Ghosts, and "Sundry Cobwebs"

1. Hearn, *Shadowings* (1900; reprint, Rutland, Vt.: Charles E. Tuttle, 1971), 222.

2. Freud, "Creative Writers and Day-Dreaming," *Complete Psychological Works,* vol. 9.

3. Hearn, Letter to Mason, 1892, *Writings,* 16:316.

4. *History of English Literature,* 2:889, 887.

5. Hearn, Letter to Chamberlain, 1 September 1893, *Writings,* 16:20.

6. [William Dean Howells] review of *Youma: The Story of a West-Indian Slave, Harper's Magazine* 81 (September 1890): 642.

7. "A Ghost" (1889), in *Karma, and Other Stories,* 63. Warner Berthoff quotes this passage in his brief but insightful commentary on Hearn in *The Ferment of Realism: American Literature, 1884–1919* (New York: Free Press, 1965), 80. Harry Levin also quotes from the passage and uses "civilized nomad" in his title of a review essay on Hearn (*New Republic* [22 April 1946]: 588–89).

8. Hearn, Autobiographical fragment, *Writings,* 13:15.

9. *Gleanings in Buddha-Fields,* 48.

10. *Japan,* 33. See the discussion of other aspects of Spencer on Japanese civilization—and of a letter by Spencer to Meiji officials—in chapter 6.

11. At the Hearn centennial celebration in Matsue (September 1990), two of his stories from *Kwaidan* (1904) were presented as Kabuki plays. In a sense this represented a return of his materials to original forms.

12. James Michener, *The Hokusai Sketchbooks: Selections from the Manga* (Rutland, Vt.: Charles E. Tuttle, 1958). The chapter "Grotesqueries" begins on p. 195.

13. Despite its specific emphasis on the visual and theatrical arts, *Japanese Ghosts and Demons: Art of the Supernatural* (ed. Stephen Addiss [New York: George Braziller, 1985]), offers excellent accounts of demonic and ghostly traditions.

14. See Hearn's defense of the ukiyo-e tradition in "About Faces in Japanese Art" (*Gleanings in Buddha-Fields*), which essentially deprecates modern Western realism and its supporters in both Japan and the West.

15. See, for example, Terence Barrow's fine introduction to *Japanese Grotesqueries,* comp. Nikolas Kiej'e (Rutland, Vt.: Charles E. Tuttle, 1973), 14.

16. See Ellen Pifer's "Shades of Love: Nabokov's Intimations of Immortality," *Kenyon Review* 11 (Spring 1989): 75–86.

17. These are Berthoff's words in *Ferment of Realism,* 81.

18. Hearn, *Some Chinese Ghosts* (Boston: Roberts Brothers, 1887).

19. *Kwaidan,* xv.

20. Hearn, *Stray Leaves from Strange Literature: Stories Reconstructed from the Anvari-Soheili, Baital, Pachisi, Mahabharata, Pantchantra, Gulistan, Talmud, Kalewala, Etc.* (Boston: J. R. Osgood, 1884).

21. Maxine Hong Kingston, *The Woman Warrior: Memoirs of a Girlhood among Ghosts* (New York: Alfred A. Knopf, 1976).

22. See, for example, Brenda Jordan's "*Yurei:* Tales of Female Ghosts," in Addiss, *Japanese Ghosts and Demons,* esp. 33. Japanese officials themselves worried about the power of ghost stories and in 1808 banned certain

kinds (Kiej'e, *Japanese Grotesqueries*, 18). On the issue of meaning and morality in Western fairy tales, see Bruno Bettelheim's *The Uses of Enchantment* (New York: Alfred A. Knopf, 1986): "More can be learned from them [fairy tales] about the inner problems of human beings, and the right solution to their predicaments . . . than from any other type of story within a child's comprehension" (5). Hearn also argued the importance of the emotional effects of reading on children.

23. Hearn, *Kwaidan*, 211.

24. Marcel Robert, "Matsue," *Lafcadio Hearn*, intro. *Selected Writings*, xviii.

25. Hearn, *History of English Literature*, 2:780.

26. *Kwaidan*, iii–iv.

27. *Glimpses*, 637–38, in the chapter "Of Ghosts and Goblins"; see also *Writings*, 15:378.

28. For Hearn's place in the history of folklore, see W. K. McNeil, "Lafcadio Hearn, American Folklorist," *Journal of American Folklore* 91 (October–December 1978): 947–67.

29. Earl R. Miner, *The Japanese Tradition*, 29.

30. Hearn, "The Story of Mimi-Nashi-Hoichi"; "The Story of O-Tei"; "The Story of Aoyagi," *Kwaidan*, 3, 29, 121.

31. "Yuki Onna," *Kwaidan*, 111.

32. "Horai," *Kokoro: Hints and Echoes of Japanese Inner Life* (1896; repr. Rutland, Vt.: Charles E. Tuttle, 1972), 29.

33. "Hi-Mawari," *Kwaidan*, 165, 166, 167.

34. *Stories from Pierre Loti*, 226.

35. Edith Wharton, *The Collected Short Stories*, ed. and intro. R. W. B. Lewis, 2 vols. (New York: Scribner's 1968), 2:876.

36. Hearn, "A Ghost," *Karma*, 65.

37. "Hi-Mawari," *Kwaidan*, 169, 70.

38. Among a number of studies of the uncanny in American and British literature, see Allan Gardner Lloyd-Smith, *Uncanny American Fiction: Medusa's Face* (New York: St. Martin's Press, 1989). Lloyd-Smith does not mention Hearn.

39. Freud, "Das Unheimliche" ["The Uncanny"], *Complete Psychological Works*, 17:249.

40. William Wordsworth, *The Prelude, 1799, 1805, 1850*, ed. Jonathan Wordsworth, M. H. Abrams, Stephen Gill (New York: Norton, 1979), 95.

5. Western Critic in an Eastern World

Epigraph: Hearn, *Talks to Writers* [selections from Hearn's lectures], ed. John Erskine (New York: Dodd, Mead, 1920), 173.

1. *Talks to Writers*, 231.

2. Hearn, *Articles on Literature and Other Writings from the Cincin-*

nati "Enquirer" (New York: AMS, 1975), 24; *History of English Literature*, 2:190, 780.

3. Letter to Chamberlain, 22 February 1894, *Writings*, 16:130.

4. See John J. Espey, "The Two Japans of Lafcadio Hearn," *Pacific Spectator* 4, no. 3 (1950). Espey points out how much of Hearn's basic commentary on the state of the "new Japan" began with assessments of its educational conditions (342).

5. "Report on the Teaching of English during the Third Term of the Academic Year, 1896–97, to M. Toyama of Imperial University," in *Some New Letters*, 424–25. Elizabeth Stevenson managed to see this as "a confident, tactful report" of the year's work (*Lafcadio Hearn*, 294).

6. *Stenographic Records*, esp. 2–4.

7. Edward Thomas, *Lafcadio Hearn*, 111. Although one of Thomas's many potboilers of the time, his study reflects a subtle and appreciative mind.

8. Hajime Matsuura, *Stenographic Records*, 8.

9. See, for example, Hachisaburo Fujisaki, in *Stenographic Records*, 37.

10. Naosaburo Hirota, *Stenographic Records*, 94.

11. Letter to Mitchell McDonald, February 1899, *Writings*, 15:165–66.

12. Hearn wrote of Hawthorne's *Septimius Felton* that it "should not have been published,—because the author had neither finished nor corrected the manuscript at the time of his death" (*History of English Literature*, 2:892).

13. There have been various collections of Hearn's lectures. *A History of English Literature* is the most definitive, along with *Complete Lectures on Poetry* (Hokuseido, 1934), hereafter cited as *On Poetry*; *Complete Lectures on Poets* (Hokuseido, 1934), hereafter cited as *On Poets*; and *On Art, Literature, and Philosophy* (Hokuseido, 1941), all edited by R. Tanabe, T. Ochiai, and I. Nishizaki. I have also used other collections, including those by John Erskine, cited elsewhere.

14. Hearn, *Pre-Raphaelite and Other Poets*, comp. and ed. John Erskine (New York: Dodd, Mead, 1922), vii–viii.

15. In his *The Memory of Certain Persons* (New York: J. B. Lippincott, 1947), John Erskine says: "It seemed to me, reading his lectures for the first time, that he equaled the best of English critics, and perhaps surpassed them all" (237).

16. Beongcheon Yu cites these and other opinions in "Toward World Literature," *An Ape of Gods: The Art and Thought of Lafcadio Hearn* (Detroit: Wayne State University Press, 1964), 167–82.

17. Yu, *Ape of Gods*, esp. chap. 9.

18. John Erskine, ed. and intro., *Interpretations of Literature*, by Lafcadio Hearn, 2 vols. (New York: Dodd, Mead, 1915), 1:5.

19. Quoted by Erskine, *Interpretations*, 1:viii.

20. Cited in Chris Baldick, *The Social Mission of English Criticism*,

1848–1932 (New York: Oxford, 1983), 88–89.

21. Hearn, *History of English Literature*, 1:239, 2:238.

22. Hearn, *Lectures on Shakespeare*, ed. Iwao Inagaki (Tokyo: Hokuseido, 1928), 47–48; *History of English Literature*, 1:113.

23. *On Poetry*, 638–39.

24. *Talks to Writers*, 153.

25. *Lectures on Shakespeare*, 6.

26. Hearn, *Some Strange English Literary Figures*, ed. R. Tanabe (Tokyo: Hokuseido, 1926), 66, 72.

27. *Some Strange Figures*, 80.

28. *On Poets*, 800.

29. *History of English Literature*, 2:866–67.

30. *History of English Literature*, 2:889.

31. *History of English Literature*, 2:877, 883.

32. Ray McKinley Lawless, *Lafcadio Hearn: Critic of American Life and Letters* (Chicago: University of Chicago Press, 1942), 29.

33. Hearn, *On Poets*, 823; *Writings*, 13:263–69.

34. *On Poets*, 840.

35. *History*, 2:733; *Victorian Philosophy* (Tokyo: Hokuseido, 1930), 1.

36. See Paul Zweig, *Walt Whitman: The Making of the Poet* (New York: Basic Books, 1984), 132.

37. Hearn, Letter to Ernest Crosby, August 1904, *Writings*, 15:253.

38. *Victorian Philosophy*, 5.

39. Letter to Page M. Baker, August 1891, *Writings*, 14:147.

40. Letter to Ellwood Hendrick, April 1892, *Writings*, 14:190. It is "utterly impossible," he says in 1895 to Chamberlain, that the Japanese "can ever reach our aesthetic stage" (321–22).

41. *On Poets*, 676.

42. *Writings*, 14:85; letter to Chamberlain, 26 January 1894, in Barrett.

43. *History of English Literature*, esp. 1:28, 45.

44. *Stenographic Records*, 21. See also Hearn's letters to students, in which he disparages "the professions of literature and teaching" (Letter to Masanobu Otani, 4 March 1894, *Some New Letters*, 198).

45. Hearn, *Letters from the Raven*, 99.

46. Earl R. Miner's "The Technique of Japanese Poetry," *Hudson Review* 8, no. 3 (Autumn 1955), 350–66, though far more technical than Hearn's discussions, offers the same kind of sympathetic insights.

47. Erskine, intro., *Interpretations*, 9.

6. Hearn and Japanese Civilization

Epigraphs: Letter of July 1887, *Newly Discovered Letters from Hearn to Matas*, 92; Herman Melville, *Moby-Dick, or, The Whale*, ed. Harrison Hayford, Hershel Parker, G. Thomas Tanselle (Evanston: Northwestern University Press, 1988), chap. III, p. 482.

1. For a discussion of Japanese estimates of the West, see Masao Miyoshi's *As We Saw Them: The First Japanese Embassy to the United States (1860)* (Berkeley: University of California Press, 1979).

2. The writer was a mariner, James Brooke: quoted in V. G. Kiernan's informative study of colonialism, *The Lords of Human Kind: Black Man, Yellow Man, and White Man in an Age of Empire* (Boston: Little, Brown, 1969), 171.

3. The best introduction to nineteenth-century anthropology is the History of Anthropology Series of the University of Wisconsin Press; see also George W. Stocking, Jr.'s, *Race, Culture, and Evolution: Essays in the History of Anthropology* (New York: Free Press, 1968); and, above all, his *Victorian Anthropology* (New York: Free Press, 1987).

4. Ruth Benedict, *The Chrysanthemum and the Sword: Patterns of Japanese Culture* (Boston: Houghton Mifflin, 1946).

5. See the discussion of Fenollosa in Chisolm, *Fenollosa.*

6. For general backgrounds on imperialism and its relation to "culture," see, for example, Patrick Brantlinger, *Rule of Darkness: British Literature and Imperialism, 1830–1914* (Ithaca: Cornell University Press, 1988).

7. See, for example, Charles MacFarlane, *Japan: An Account* (Hartford, Conn.: Silas Andrus, 1856). I am indebted here to Miner's *Japanese Tradition,* 9–30.

8. Sir Edwin Arnold, *Japonica* (New York: Scribner's, 1892).

9. Ernest Fenollosa, "East and West," *East and West: The Discovery of America and Other Poems* (1893; reprint, Upper Saddle River, N.J.: Literature House, 1970), 5–6.

10. Ernest Fenollosa, "Fuji at Sunrise," quoted in Miner, *Japanese Tradition,* 33.

11. Hearn, "Revery," *Kotto.*

12. "A Woman's Diary," *Kotto.* This work is dedicated to Sir Edwin Arnold.

13. Hearn, "China and the Western World," *Karma,* 452.

14. Max Weber, *The Protestant Ethic and the Spirit of Capitalism,* trans. Talcott Parsons (1904–5; reprint, New York: Free Press, 1958). Weber speaks of the entire "rationalization of Western culture" (xv).

15. Hearn, *Japan, Writings,* 12:461. The letters to Japan can be found in David Duncan, *Life and Letters of Herbert Spencer,* 2 vols. (New York: D. Appleton, 1908), 2:11–18.

16. Hearn, "Notes of a Trip to Izumo," *Atlantic Monthly* (1897), reprinted in *Lands and Seas,* comp. T. Ochiai (Tokyo: Hokuseido, 1925).

17. Hearn, *The Romance of the Milky Way, and Other Studies and Stories* (1905; reprint, Rutland, Vt.: Charles E. Tuttle, 1973). The volume appeared the year following Hearn's death. Of particular interest is the final section, "A Letter from Japan," dated 1 August 1904 and dealing with the war against Russia.

18. *Editorials from the Kobe "Chronicle."* A large number of the edi-

torials were collected by P. D. Perkins but not published; they are available in typescript in the Barrett collection.

19. *Japan*, 18, 33.

20. *Japan*, 16.

21. *Glimpses*, 143; Notebook, 1890–91, 36, in Barrett.

22. Hans Jonas, *The Gnostic Religion* (Boston: Beacon Press, 1963), 45. Jonas is translating from an ancient text.

23. Hearn, Letter to Bisland, 1890, in *Writings*, 14:104.

24. Walt Whitman, "A Broadway Pageant" (1860), *Leaves of Grass*, 243–45.

25. Hearn, *Glimpses*, 10; *Japan*, 119.

26. *Japan*, 16–17, 18.

27. During the Second World War, William Clary wrote an article arguing that Hearn did in fact anticipate Japan's military aggression and warned the West about it ("Japan: The Warnings and Prophecies of Lafcadio Hearn," *Claremont Oriental Studies* 5 [April 1943], 1–17).

28. Hearn, *Japan*, 454.

29. Singer, *Mirror, Sword, and Jewel*.

30. T. J. Jackson Lears, *No Place of Grace: Anti-Modernism and the Transformation of American Culture, 1880–1920* (New York: Pantheon, 1981). Lears speaks of *modernist* and *antimodernist*, but the terms unfortunately have opposite meanings for historians and literary historians.

31. In addition to Said's study, *Orientalism*, see Schwab, *Oriental Renaissance;* and Kiernan, *Lords of Human Kind.*

32. See, for example, Raymond Williams, *Problems in Materialism and Culture: Selected Essays* (London: Verso Editions, 1980), 19–22.

33. See Martha Howard Sisson, *Lafcadio Hearn: A Bibliography*, reprinted from the *Bulletin of Bibliography* (Boston: F. W. Faxon, 1933). The primary bibliography is P. D. and Ione Perkins, *Lafcadio Hearn: A Bibliography of His Writings* (1934; reprint, New York: Burt Franklin, 1968).

34. James Clifford, "On Ethnographic Authority," *Representations* 1 (1983): 118–24; see also *The Predicament of Culture: Twentieth-Century Ethnography, Literature, and Art* (Cambridge: Harvard University Press, 1988), which includes the essay.

35. Hearn, Letter to Krehbiel, 1885, *Writings*, 13:334.

36. Letter of 17 July 1888, *New Hearn Letters from the French West Indies*, 78. In the context he means abilities for fiction writing.

37. At the Matsue centennial festival the distinguished Japanese scholar Hirakawa Sukehiro argued that, though Hearn's reputation among Western scholars has declined, he is still very much—and rightly—honored in Japan.

38. Koizumi, *Letter from Chamberlain to Hearn*, 120–21.

39. Hearn, *Writings*, 15:14.

40. Benedict, *Chrysanthemum*, 14.

Index

Designed by Pat Crowder

Composed by The Composing Room of Michigan, Inc., in Trump text
and display

Printed by The Maple Press Company, Inc., on 55-lb. Sebago Antique
Cream and bound in Holliston Roxite A 50264 linen finish.